"In this wonderful book Tullian creatively and clearly does with the story of Jonah what the Bible was designed to do—see yourself and weep and see your God and rejoice. Read. It will deepen your sense of need and your affection for the God who meets you in the middle of it."

PAUL TRIPP, President, Paul Tripp Ministries

"*Surprised by Grace* fishes the gospel from the storms of Jonah's life and conscience with wonderful images from art history, beautiful words from classic literature, and deep insight from the biblical record. The ways Pastor Tullian shows how the gospel spouts from so ancient—and resistant—a prophet is truly a surprising grace."

BRYAN CHAPELL, President, Covenant Theological Seminary

"If you've been struggling with the Christian faith because it started with the gospel and moved quickly into the 'elbow grease' of hard work, guilt, and rules, this book will change your life. The gospel isn't just where we begin; it's where we Christians live. If we aren't surprised by grace, it isn't grace. Read this book, and you'll rise up and call me blessed for recommending it to you."

STEVE BROWN, author, *A Scandalous Freedom: The Radical Nature of the* Gospel; host, *Key Life*

"Tullian has given us a crash course on the outrageous mathematics of God's mercy and grace. The same God who pursues violent pagan kings also pursues his smug, self-righteous sons and daughters. Indeed, the God who bids us count stars, sand, and dust is actively redeeming a pan-national family of rebels, idolaters, and broken people just like me . . . and you! Thanks, Tullian, for helping me to see that the gospel is always bigger than I realized, or even wanted it to be!"

SCOTTY SMITH, Pastor for Preaching, Teaching, and Worship, Christ Community Church, Franklin, Tennessee

"*Surprised by Grace* will delight many, and it will disturb some. The gospel does that. Tullian Tchividjian helps us all, as sinners, move the gospel down into our hearts, where we actually change. Thank you, Tullian. I need it. Everyone on the face of the earth needs it."

RAY ORTLUND, Lead Pastor, Immanuel Church, Nashville, Tennessee

"Tullian's masterful retelling of this familiar story will do just as it promises. It will surprise you—shock you even—as you hear the story of Jonah as if for the first time. And it will fill you with awe and wonder at God's startling grace and his tender heart toward us, his lost and rebellious children. I loved it."

SALLY LLOYD-JONES, author, *The Jesus Story-Book Bible: Every Story Whispers His Name*

"The book of Jonah is more than the story of a prophet who ran from God. It is actually the story of the grace of God that overcomes Jonah's stubborn rebellion. In this outstanding book Tchividjian helps us see that there is something of Jonah in all of us and that we stand in need of the same grace of God every day. I was both convicted and encouraged by this book and highly recommend it to every Christian."

JERRY BRIDGES, author, *The Pursuit of Holiness*

"*Surprised by Grace* is much-needed reminder that we should never get over the gospel or try to move beyond it. The grace that saves is the grace that satisfies and empowers. Tullian's book is gospel-saturated, Christ-exalting, and soul-refreshing."

RANDY ALCORN, author, *Heaven* and *If God Is Good*

"Twenty years ago Tullian was the wild, rebellious black sheep among Billy Graham's grandchildren. Today he follows in his grandfather's steps as a powerful preacher of the cross of Christ. As he retells the Old Testament story of Jonah, he shows that while sin reaches far, God's grace reaches farther. Tullian's heart to see rebels—as well as cold-hearted Pharisees—transformed by the gospel of grace shines through on every page."

JOSHUA HARRIS, Pastor, Covenant Life Church, Gaithersburg, Maryland; author, *Dug Down Deep*

"A well-written, exegetically careful, pastorally sensitive journey through a familiar yet surprising book. Tullian mines the world of literature, art, and theology to bring out the abiding significance of this beloved story. Oh, and he also wonderfully points us to Christ."

KEVIN DEYOUNG, Senior Pastor, University Reformed Church, East Lansing, Michigan; author, *The Good News We Almost Forgot: Rediscovering the Gospel in a 16th Century Catechism*

"As one who is both self-righteously religious and rebelliously irreligious (and sometimes on the same day!), I am repeatedly surprised by God's relentless pursuit of my heart and his overwhelming grace. I'm sure that Tchividjian's transparent interaction with a heartless prophet who is nevertheless an instrument of mercy to a wicked, godless nation will both convict and comfort you as it did me. In this wonderful book you'll learn that Jonah's story is not so much the story of a runaway prophet, a fish, a vine, and a repenting nation as it is a story of God's persistent purpose to bless people he chooses to bless, no matter the cost. If you need to remember that God is greater than your sin, that his purpose to bless isn't really dependent upon your goodness, and that he will accomplish all his purposes no matter what, this Christ-exalting book will serve you well. It's just splendid."

ELYSE FITZPATRICK, author, *Because He Loves Me: How Christ Transforms Our Daily Life*

"Calvin called Scripture a 'mirror of the soul.' Tullian Tchividjian's insightful guidance through the book of Jonah not only clearly explains the meaning of the book but helps us see ourselves in the reluctant prophet, sinners who are the recipients of God's loving grace. I highly recommend *Surprised by Grace* for all Christians."

TREMPER LONGMAN, Robert H. Gundry Professor of Biblical Studies, Westmont College; author, *Reading the Bible with Heart and Mind*

"Grace is one of those words we use so much that it's easy to take for granted. It becomes ordinary. However, in this book grace shines in its biblical luster. Whether a new believer or a lifelong Christian, prepare to be surprised by grace!"

MICHAEL S. HORTON, Professor of Theology, Westminster Seminary California

"The gospel is a surprising message of news seemingly too good to be true. Tullian shocks us with the gospel as he retells the story of Jonah—the story of a God who pursues, rescues, and even uses people who run away from him. What makes this book stand out is how Tullian presents the gospel in story form, carving deep grooves in one's memory. I will not forget this book, and I will recommend it to all the 'Jonahs' in my life, which is most everybody I know."

JUSTIN BUZZARD, Pastor, Central Peninsula Church, San Francisco Bay Area; author, BuzzardBlog.com

SURPRISED *by* GRACE

GOD'S RELENTLESS PURSUIT OF REBELS

⚓

TULLIAN TCHIVIDJIAN

WHEATON, ILLINOIS

Library of Congress Cataloging-in-Publication Data
Tchividjian, Tullian.
  Surprised by grace : God's relentless pursuit of rebels / Tullian
Tchividjian.
    p. cm.
    Includes bibliographical references and index.
    ISBN 978-1-4335-0775-5 (hc)
    1. Jonah (Biblical prohet).   I. Title.
BS580.J55T43   2010
224'.9206—dc22   2009043842

To my maternal grandfather,
"Daddy Bill"

At 91 years old, God's amazing grace still amazes you—
and that amazes me!

CONTENTS

LIST OF
ILLUSTRATIONS

ACKNOWLEDGMENTS

This book started out as a series of sermons I preached during the most difficult season of my life. As I reflect on that season now, I can honestly say that I am genuinely thankful for all the pain I experienced. For it was during this trying time that God helped me recognize the practical relevance of the gospel.

Through their writing and their friendship, I am indebted to seven men in particular who, as I was preaching through Jonah, helped me make the life-saving connection between what Christ accomplished for me and my daily internal grind: Scotty Smith, Edmund Clowney, Tim Keller, Paul Tripp, Bryan Chapell, Reggie Kidd, and Jerry Bridges. These seven men have been used by God to massage the gospel deep into my bones, and I am forever grateful to them.

I'd also like to thank my good friends at Crossway for their interest in, and support of, this project from beginning to end. You are all delightful to work with!

To my editor Thomas Womack. You are simply the best. You took my transcribed sermons and turned them into a book. I thank God for your gifts. It's a great blessing to have an editor who not only understands what I'm trying to say but also agrees with me.

To my children, Gabe, Nate, and Genna. I love you all so much. It is a pure joy to be your dad. My ongoing prayer for all of you is that you would never cease to be amazed at God's surprising grace.

And, finally, to my wife, Kim. More than anyone else, you have seen the gospel of grace change my life. Thank you for your willingness to follow my lead. I love you because I love you!

We cannot find God without God.
We cannot reach God without God.

We cannot satisfy God without God—which is
another way of saying
that all our seeking will fall short unless
God starts and finishes the search.

The decisive part of our seeking is not our
human ascent to God, but his descent to us.
Without God's descent there is no human ascent.

The secret of the quest lies not in our brilliance
but in his grace.

OS GUINNESS, *Long Journey Home*

A CURE FOR GOSPEL CONFUSION

Jesus himself stood among them. . . . But they were startled.

LUKE 24:36–37

⚓

For good reason, Christian people love the word *gospel*. Tragically, however, multitudes of Christians fail to grasp what the gospel fully is. In fact, I'm convinced there's just as much confusion inside the church as there is outside it regarding the gospel's true meaning—sometimes even in churches where the gospel is regularly preached and taught.

To get a better grip on the gospel, maybe what we need most is to be startled . . . surprised . . . even *shocked* by it.

That's exactly what I believe our situation calls for. And one of the best books in the Bible for delivering such a jolt has to be Jonah—a story full of "shocking surprises and sensational elements," as one commentary puts it.[1]

And now, already, you're surprised. You're astonished that any author would offer a book-length look at Jonah for a popular audience. But for me, it was through probing this story of Jonah that I came face-to-face with one of the most life-changing truths in my experience. I came to grips with the fact that *the gospel is not just for non-Christians but also for Christians.*

THE ONLY WAY FORWARD

I once assumed the gospel was simply what non-Christians must believe in order to be saved, but after they believe it, they advance to deeper theological waters. Jonah helped me realize that the gospel isn't the first step in a stairway of truths but more like the hub in a wheel of truth. As Tim Keller explains it, the gospel isn't simply the ABCs of Christianity, but the A-through-Z. The gospel doesn't just ignite the Christian life; it's the fuel that keeps Christians going every day. Once God rescues sinners, his plan isn't to steer them beyond the gospel but to move them more deeply into it. After all, the only antidote to sin *is* the gospel—and since Christians remain sinners even after they're converted, the gospel must be the medicine a Christian takes every day. Since we never leave off sinning, we can never leave the gospel.

This idea that the gospel is just as much for Christians as for non-Christians may seem like a new idea to many, but, in fact, it is really a very old idea. In his letter to the Christians of Colossae, the apostle Paul quickly portrays the gospel as the instrument of all continued growth and spiritual progress for believers after conversion: "All over the world," he writes, "this gospel is bearing fruit and growing, just as it has been doing among you since the day you heard it and understood God's grace in all its truth" (Col. 1:6 NIV).

After meditating on Paul's words here, a friend once told me that all our problems in life stem from our failure to apply the gospel. This means we can't really move forward unless we learn more thoroughly the gospel's content and how to apply it to all of life. Real change does not and cannot come independently of the gospel, which is the good news that even though we're more defective and lost than we ever imagined, we can be more accepted and loved than we ever dared hope, because Jesus Christ lived, died, and rose again for sinners like you and me. God intends this reality to mold and shape us at every point and in every way. It should define the way we think, feel, and live.

Martin Luther often employed the phrase *simul justus et peccator* to describe his condition as a Christian. It means "simultaneously justified and sinful." He understood that while he'd already been saved (through justification) from sin's *penalty*, he was in daily need of salvation from sin's *power*. And since the gospel is the "power of God for salvation" (Rom. 1:16), he knew that even for the most saintly of saints the gospel is wholly relevant and vitally necessary—day in and day out. This means that heralded preachers need the gospel just as much as hardened pagans.

In his book *The Gospel for Real Life*, Jerry Bridges picks up on this theme—that Christians need the gospel just as much as non-Christians—by explaining how the spiritual poverty in so much of our Christian experience is the result of inadequate understanding of the gospel's depths. The answer isn't to try harder in the Christian life but to comprehend more fully and clearly Christ's incredible work on the cross, and then to live in a more vital awareness of that grace day by day. The main problem in the Christian life, in other words, is *not* that we don't try hard enough to be good. It's that we haven't thought out the deep implications of the gospel and applied its powerful reality to all parts of our life.

Sadly, many Christians have come to believe that the key to deeper spiritual renewal and revival is "working harder." The truth, however, is that *real spiritual growth happens only as we continually rediscover the gospel.*

But now you're thinking, *Is all that in the book of Jonah? Seriously?* After all, not only is Jonah almost the smallest of the Old Testament books, but its familiar story seems a bit bizarre at best. The main character, in terms of stature and reputation, probably ranks well below your favorite children's cartoon character. You're also wondering, *What could a fish-swallows-man story possibly have to do with the gospel, with being surprised by grace?*

Let me encourage you, first, to toss the notion that Jonah is primarily a story about a man gulped down by a fish. Instead, as we'll see, it's a story that essentially reveals God's heart and *ours.* What we discover about both is often startling—sometimes uncomfortably so—and perhaps no other story in the Bible sets the two in such explicit contrast.

THE GOSPEL IN STORY

To catch these things in Jonah, we have to get beyond our prior assumptions about a narrative that is "probably the best known yet least understood book in the Bible," as Ray Stedman put it.[2]

We're on the right road to better understanding it when we realize that Jonah is *a storied presentation of the gospel,* a story of sin and grace, of desperation and deliverance. It reveals the fact that while you and I are great sinners, God is a great Savior, and that while our sin reaches far, his grace reaches farther. This story shows that God is in the business of relentlessly pursuing rebels like us and that he comes after us not to angrily strip away our freedom but to affectionately strip away our slavery so we might become truly free. It's a truth reflected well in an opening line from a nineteenth-century hymn by the blind Scottish pastor George Matheson: "Make me a captive, Lord, and then I shall be free."

We'll see all those things in Jonah as we make our way attentively through this brief but profoundly dramatic and eventful account. At each phrase and image and event, we'll try to look closely enough, and linger long enough, to experience this story intensely, letting it be all that it truly is. We'll keep asking, "What's here to see and learn for both the spiritual seeker and the follower of Jesus?"

It's a story that thoroughly rewards close inspection. We'll find the book of Jonah to be a masterpiece of story art and literary design. It's "simple enough to delight a child and complex enough to confound a scholar," as one such scholar notes. "It invites reflection and contemplation on a number of important levels and themes."[3]

Because there's so much more here than anyone would typically see in just a cursory reading, I've come to deeply appreciate the book of Jonah. I can honestly say that through this book I've seen the gospel—and allowed it to work in my life—in ways I've never before experienced.

JUST HOW TRUE IS IT?

Somewhere in the back (or even the front) of your mind, maybe there's a pesky doubt about the historical accuracy of some things described in Jonah. If so, you're far from alone. The narrative recounted here "is almost incredible," Martin Luther exclaimed, "sounding more strange than any poet's fable; if it were not in the Bible, I should take it for a lie." By comparison, Luther insisted, "the wonderful passage through the Red Sea was nothing."[4]

Despite the story's implausible elements, Luther could accept its accuracy because the Bible itself presents Jonah as a factual account. Nevertheless, some scholars have found it preferable to think of it as an extended parable or allegory—meaningful, yes; factual, no. But arguments for the fictional nature of the book of Jonah lose a lot of punch in the full light of Scripture. It appears that Jesus not only considered Jonah's story to be true but emphasized its factualness. Matthew's Gospel records two occasions when the influential Jews of his day asked Jesus for some indicator of his divinity, and he answered that "the sign of Jonah" was the only notice they were getting.[5] If the story was nothing more than a fictionalized legend, its value as a "sign" would seem questionable.

Jesus also bluntly promised his listeners their own future encounter with the very people Jonah had preached to centuries earlier. Jesus assured the Jews of his day that the Ninevites will "rise up at the judgment" to condemn them. Such a claim on the Lord's part would seem rather dishonest—empty and even ridiculous—if Jonah's story was merely an imaginary tale.

I believe that once we examine this story more closely and humbly—with an open heart and eyes of faith, ready to be taught by the Holy Spirit—not only will we reap the deeper lessons it gives, but we'll see that the whole thing "rings true" more and more. We'll recognize that the very outlandishness of these strange events was part of God's purpose and design.

That's just the kind of thing it takes to really shock our senses so that our eyes are opened to what God wants us to see.

HEARING THE SAVIOR'S VOICE

Taking their cue from Jesus, the courageous Christians in the church's early centuries attached great importance to Jonah's story, embracing its surprises and delighting in their truthfulness. Images from Jonah's story are common, for example, in the Roman catacombs from that era. Those believers especially rejoiced in the "sign of Jonah" that pointed to Christ's resurrection from the grave.

One art historian notes that Jonah's story was among the four most popular Old Testament themes in early Christian art (the other three were Adam and Eve, Abraham's offering of Isaac, and Daniel in the lions' den).[6] Elements of Jonah's story and Christ's story are often juxtaposed in this art, hinting at how clearly and easily the early believers connected the two.

On the ceiling in one Roman catacomb, a figure of Christ the Good Shepherd is encircled by illustrations of the Jonah story. These are interspersed with separate figures of a man, a woman, and a child with arms raised in prayer—a cross-section of the Christian family seeking a heavenly afterlife.[7] Those early believers seemed to relish the story of Jonah because they kept hearing in it the voice of their resurrected Savior and Shepherd.

As the centuries went by, the story of Jonah maintained its notable place in humanity's art and imagination, though doubts about its veracity were always present among unbelievers. In AD 409, Augustine mentioned how the story was "a laughing stock of the Pagans," as he replied to a letter from someone who described it as "improbable and unbelievable."[8] Improbable it was, but artists and poets still kept imagining and interacting with Jonah's story. It was just so engaging and unforgettable.

Even in recent centuries, as skepticism and cynicism have taken ever-deeper root, the story has stayed in our culture's conscience—yes, often laughed at and disbelieved, and commonly misunderstood even when believed, but never forgotten.

In these pages, I encourage you to enter Jonah's story with fresh eyes. Come to it as if for the very first time, to let the story be exactly what it is, and all that it is. And may you—like your Christian brothers and sisters of so long ago—come to hear in it the welcome, unmistakable sound of your Good Shepherd's voice and thus grow more confident than ever about what the gospel is and how it works.

PART ONE

A DEADLY PLUNGE

⚓

The Story's Beginning
GOD CALLS

*Now therefore, if you will indeed obey my voice . . . you shall be
my treasured possession.*

EXODUS 19:5

⚓

To know Jonah is to love him," writes Lloyd John Ogilvie. "And the reason we love him is because he is so much like us in our response to God's guidance."[1] The man Jonah is indeed like us in a number of ways. Learning to identify with him is our key to the meaning of his story—and our big mistake if we fail to do so. As Ogilvie suggests, we pick up a great deal from this book about God's guidance and about discovering his will. We learn about the danger we experience when we run from God's will, the deliverance we experience when we submit to God's will, the deliverance *others* experience when we fulfill God's will, and the depression we experience when we question God's will.

But the book of Jonah is about much more than discovering the will of God for us as individuals, as we'll see while getting to know this surprising story more intimately.

A SUCCESSFUL PROPHET'S RÉSUMÉ

If this guy Jonah is like you and me, it isn't so obvious as we begin his story:

Now the word of the LORD came to Jonah the son of Amittai.
(1:1)

Hearing or reading those opening words, the initial audience for the book of Jonah would have recognized immediately the biblical ring to them, because the same phrasing is so commonly attached to names like Samuel and Elijah. Like those men, but unlike you and me, Jonah is *a prophet of the Lord God.*

What else do we know about this prophet? Christians who feel well acquainted with Jonah's story often are surprised to learn that his background is mentioned earlier in the Bible, in the book of 2 Kings. There we read that Jonah had experienced a rare treat for a Hebrew prophet: he foretold something good for the nation of Israel, then saw it quickly happen.

It was during the days of Israel's King Jeroboam II, who reigned over the northern kingdom of Israel in the first half of the eighth century BC. This king beefed up a long section of Israel's northern border, strengthening its defense against any potential Assyrian invaders. King Jeroboam did this not just to implement his own military strategy, but, by the gracious prompting of God, he did it "according to the word of the LORD, the God of Israel, which he spoke *by his servant Jonah the son of Amittai,* the prophet, who was from Gath-hepher" (2 Kings 14:25).

Restoring this border was more than a mere maintenance measure. It was a critically urgent accomplishment in a moment of profound national need, as we quickly sense from the next verses: "For the LORD saw that the affliction of Israel was very bitter . . . and there was none to help Israel." God made it clear that he would *not* "blot out the name of Israel from under heaven, so he saved them by the hand of Jeroboam" (14:26–27).

So God truly cared for Israel, enough to act immediately—through its king—to fortify its national defenses. And Jonah had been given the privilege of conveying this good news to his countrymen. Here was a deliberate act of the Lord's deliverance; by this "he *saved* them."

Jonah must have won lasting fame after uttering this prophecy and quickly seeing it come to fruition through King Jeroboam's capable military leadership. The prophet had spoken, and what he'd spoken came to pass—the ultimate professional test for any prophet.

All this must only have intensified Jonah's sense of national and spiritual pride as a son of Israel. If God relied on popular tastes and consumer demand in crafting the books in his Scriptures, he might well have pulled together an inspiring tale about Jonah the hero from this particular setting and time period instead of giving us the story we have from later on. (Jonah might have liked it better that way too!)

It's also worth noting in this 2 Kings passage that Jonah "was from Gath-hepher," a town in Galilee in the heart of the northern kingdom, just three miles from where another Galilean, the carpenter Jesus, would grow up in Nazareth many years later.

Five centuries ago, the Renaissance painter Raphael created a brown-wash-on-black-chalk drawing of Jonah that seems to capture well how the prophet might have looked at this stage in his career.[2] In typical Raphael style, Jonah looks gracefully heroic. The sturdy hand of his downward-stretched left arm grips the top of a stone tablet resting on the thigh of his thrust-forward leg. Against his broad chest, his right hand grips the folds of his flowing mantle, which drapes his muscular shoulders.

Jonah's face—with a short beard, fine nose, full cheeks, and a mature, receding hairline—is turned over his left shoulder. His eyes gaze behind him and upward, as if at that very moment he's hearing from heaven "the word of the LORD" that "came to Jonah the son of Amittai."

Is this the moment when he's given God's message of mercy for strengthening Israel's borders? Or is it the much different calling that this successful prophet receives as the book of Jonah opens?

ARISE AND GO

Right away we encounter the first in a nonstop string of big surprises in this book, each one often topping the previous one in shock value.

> Now the word of the LORD came to Jonah the son of Amittai, saying, "Arise, go to Nineveh, that great city, and call out against it, for their evil has come up before me." (1:1–2)

Many Old Testament prophets were given a word to speak "against" the surrounding powers and empires of those centuries. But to actually be *sent* to one of them to give God's judgment-message by personal delivery—that just wasn't part of a prophet's normal job description.

Jonah's assigned destination could not have been more imposing. He knows that the city of Nineveh is indeed "great"; the Hebrew word here is *gadol*, and it's a major theme-word we'll see again and again in key descriptions in Jonah. Nineveh—

large, populous, well fortified—is the leading city in Assyria, the greatest world power of that day and the most disturbing long-term threat to Israel's security and survival.

Moreover, Nineveh is the reigning "sin city." Perhaps Jonah already knows that, but more important is the reminder that God himself is very personally aware of it: "Their evil," he says, "has come up *before me*."

That's the place to which Jonah is to arise and go and to "cry against it." The assignment probably takes his breath away. Jonah may already be a homeland hero due to his prophetic success toward building Israel's defenses, but if that means anything at all in proud, idolatrous Nineveh, it can only be a strike against him.

A PROPHET PREPARED

John Calvin's landmark commentary on the book of Jonah has long been a classic. Throughout its pages, the Reformer repeatedly shows keen sensitivity and sympathy toward Jonah and his condition, even while promptly exposing the man's flaws and shame. Calvin points to God's particular grace toward Jonah in reminding him of Nineveh's greatness. Since men often undertake a huge task boldly enough, only to wilt later on when unforeseen difficulties batter them, perhaps God is getting everything out on the table for his prophet—setting him up for no surprises. God "intended thus to prepare him with firmness,"[3] Calvin suggests, lest Jonah be overwhelmed by the magnitude of Nineveh's power and population, and of her wealth and wickedness.

God's gracious provision also seems to be behind his statement that Nineveh's evil "has come up before me." Jonah will be only the instrument, the messenger; the issue to resolve is really between *God* and Nineveh, and God, of course, can easily handle that. It's as if, Calvin says, the Lord is telling Jonah, "Remember who I am, and be content with my authority; for I have ready at hand all resources; when anything stands in your way, rely on my power, and execute what I commanded thee."[4]

This book's original audience, hearing or reading those opening two verses in Jonah for the first time, might immediately have high expectations about what should come next. Will it be a thrilling scene-by-scene unfolding of how an obedient messenger courageously carries God's warning to the very face of his enemies—followed up perhaps by plenty of wrath-of-God fireworks?

But already we're in for a second huge surprise in this narrative.

GOING, GONE

Our story's main character definitely fails to follow the protocol for prophets.

> But Jonah rose to flee to Tarshish from the presence of the LORD. He went down to Joppa and found a ship going to Tarshish. So he paid the fare and went on board, to go with them to Tarshish, away from the presence of the LORD. (1:3)

The repeated phrase here is stunning, even haunting in effect: he "rose to flee . . . *from the presence of the LORD.* . . . *Away from the presence of the LORD.*" The additional details here smack of deliberate, headlong intention: Jonah gets up to flee, sets out for the seaport, locates a ship, pays his passage, and gets on board to *go.* There's no doubt about it: this guy's determined to ditch

God—the same God who declares, "Do I not fill heaven and earth?" (Jer. 23:24). How senseless and stupid, especially for a prophet of the Lord!

Here we first witness in this book the jarring mix of the ridiculous with utterly serious reality, a mingling that will continue throughout. Jonah's reaction appears so rash and irrational. An African-American minstrel song of the 1800s summed up his behavior this way:

> Jonah was a fool
> and as stubborn as a mule.[5]

Couldn't he at least try to reason with God, like Moses did at the burning bush while protesting his lack of oratory skills for leading the Hebrews out of Egypt, or like Elijah did in the wilderness, bemoaning his aloneness while on the run from Jezebel and Ahab?

Yet, on further reflection, we can find plausible explanations for Jonah's response. On the face of it, his flight seems only to underscore the daunting massiveness of what he'll encounter if he does what he's been asked to do. Don't forget that this story is *real:* Nineveh's hugeness and wickedness are real; God's aggrieved warning is real; Jonah's assignment to proclaim that warning is real. Would you or I launch eagerly into such a task?

DISTURBED, CONFUSED, BLINDED

It's easy to perceive the character of Jonah too one-dimensionally and to fall short of engaging all that's here. After all, this is a pretty fast read; as one commentary reminds us, the book of Jonah "is straightforward narrative that is remarkable for its lack of background and unnecessary detail."[6] There's no fluff here. But what *is* here is a gold mine. Every line and phrase has weight and purpose that contribute to the intended effect. And when all these details and their implications are fully reckoned with, they reveal Jonah as a forceful and complex personality with apparent strengths as well as crucial flaws.

Nevertheless, as understandable as Jonah's reaction may be, and as easy as it is to find excuses for it (especially considering our own fears and failures), we aren't told—*yet*—exactly why Jonah is fleeing. For now, it's an open question, almost as if the narrative is inviting our natural and logical assumptions while we wait for Jonah's own explanation, which will come only after a long and traumatic ordeal for him.

Calvin, with characteristic sympathy mixed with blunt assessment, suggests that Jonah was plagued by hopelessness and despair about his assignment, plus "weakness of the flesh" and more: "He was, no doubt, not only in a disturbed state of mind . . . but was utterly confused."[7] However, none of those factors add up to a suitable defense before God. The fact is, Jonah the escapist has "grievously transgressed," as Calvin concludes. "He could not have sinned more grievously than by forsaking God, in having refused to obey his call"; he was being led by "perverse and blind impulse."[8] In time, we'll learn much about the exact nature of his blindness.

HIS OWN GOD

To flee from God is to rise against God. It is stand-up, straight-out, in-your-face defiance against the One to whom we owe all loyalty and love. It means insisting that our way of doing things is better than God's way.

That's why, if we're honest, we can start already to identify with Jonah. His runaway posture is *our* posture, *every time we sin*, whether in thought, word, or deed, whether it's something we consider big or something small, whether it's doing something we shouldn't or failing to do something we should. Every time we sin, we're telling God, "My way of navigating this particular situation is better than yours. My wisdom and skill are more efficient and more effective in this moment than your wisdom and skill." It's not that we stop believing. It's just that *what* we believe has shifted.

In one of G. K. Chesterton's famous Father Brown detective stories, the main character addresses some self-described "materialists" with these words: "As a matter of fact you were all balanced on the very edge of belief—of belief in almost anything. There are thousands balanced on it today; but it's a sharp, uncomfortable edge to sit on. You won't rest till you believe *something*."[9] When we sin, that something which we choose to believe in is not *no God*, but *ourselves as god*. Like Adam and Eve, each time we sin we're choosing to be our own deity. We're placing ultimate trust in ourselves, not in our Creator and Savior and Lord.

Do you know what would happen if every human being concluded that God's way was the right way and God's call the right call? Every human problem would come to an end. The root of every human problem is our desire to be our own god and to carry out justice in the way we ourselves are sure is best.

In all of human history, there has been only One who concluded—at every point, and in every way—that God's way is always best and God's call is always right. Because of him, every human problem will someday come to an end. In the meantime, we'll never see the end of our own misery if we do not recognize Jesus, this one who so perfectly submitted to God's way and God's call.

SHADOWS AND SUBSTANCE

It's right here that we start seeing Jesus in the Jonah story. We make a huge mistake if we think we don't really come across Jesus in the Bible until we reach the New Testament and the Gospels. We encounter him first in Genesis 1, when God the Father, God the Son, and God the Holy Spirit come together for the purpose of creating everything out of nothing. Then we see Jesus again in Genesis 3, when God promises that a seed from the woman will crush the serpent's head. All the rest of the Old Testament—including the book of Jonah—continues to build on that promise.

In seminary I had a professor who referred to the New Testament as the Bible's footnotes. He meant no disrespect; he knew the New Testament is just as inspired and trustworthy and infallible as the Old. He was simply saying in a different way what Augustine said centuries earlier—that the New Testament is contained in the Old, and the Old Testament is explained in the New.[10]

The New Testament adds the color for the black-and-white picture we've already been given in the Old Testament. In the Old Testament God reveals his Messiah in promises, in prophecies, and in shadows. In the New Testament we discover that Jesus is the fulfillment of every promise and prophecy, and the substance behind every shadow. And we'll find some of those shadows right here in Jonah.

THIS COULD BE THE END

In running from the Lord, Jonah is choosing to be his own god. He knows the Lord God but doesn't agree with what God is doing. He's placing ultimate trust in himself, not in the One who has called him to Nineveh, and, as we'll see, there's nothing more eternally dangerous than becoming our own god.

This could well have been the end of Jonah's story, right here after three verses. *This man Jonah is history*, we might conclude. *He's washed up. As a prophet and a servant of God, he's through. God will simply have to raise up another messenger to send to Nineveh.*

But there's so much more to it than that. God—and this story—continue to be full of surprises.

Scene 1:
IN A GREAT STORM

As a father shows compassion to his children,
so the LORD shows compassion to those who fear him.

PSALM 103:13

⚓

Many artists in recent times have continued turning to Jonah as a favorite biblical subject. One of the most memorable portraits of the prophet is by the Israeli artist David Sharir, done in 1971.[1] In the upper right corner is a simple, stylized cargo ship, its hold filled with wares. On deck stands the solitary figure of Jonah, carrying luggage in each hand. His wide eyes look forward. What destiny awaits him? He looks unsure.

Behind and below him, a bordered box across the bottom of the artwork encloses an ancient city packed tightly with buildings, roofs, archways. The city looks sizable and cosmopolitan. Is this the seaport Joppa from which Jonah departs? Or rather, could it represent Nineveh—from which the prophet wants to be as far away as possible? Meanwhile, between Jonah's boat in the upper corner and the crowded city down below, the biggest part of the painting is taken up with the blue immensity of the sea, as if it's waiting to play a much bigger part in Jonah's story.

SKULKING FROM GOD

The sea has a starring role as well in Herman Melville's classic novel *Moby Dick,* which happens to contain perhaps the most extensive and compelling treatment of the Jonah story in all of secular literature.

The narrator, a wandering sailor named Ishmael, arrives one December night at the whaling port of New Bedford, Massachusetts, eager to join his first whaling voyage. The next day—a cold, wet Sunday—Ishmael goes to the Whaleman's Chapel in New Bedford. Inside, sitting silently and mostly apart from each other, are fishermen bound for distant oceans as well as widows of men lost at sea. They stare at the chapel's walls, lined with black-bordered marble memorials to the sea's victims.

In time, the elderly chaplain—a former harpooner named Mapple—enters the chapel and takes off his sleet-covered hat and jacket. He climbs a rope ladder into a lofty pulpit, like mounting a platform on a ship's mast.

Mapple's sermon is from the book of Jonah, "one of the smallest strands in the mighty cable of the Scriptures," he says. "Yet what depths of the soul does Jonah's deep sea-line sound!"

The chaplain says Jonah found God's instructions to be "a hard command. But all the things that God would have us do are hard." The reason? "If we obey God, we must disobey ourselves; and it is in this disobeying ourselves, wherein the hardness of obeying God consists." Mapple grasps well the truth that our sins are always our instinctive attempt to make ourselves god.

With striking creative powers, the preacher portrays Jonah as he "skulks about the wharves of Joppa" and "seeks a ship that's bound for Tarshish." Tarshish, the chaplain explains, is probably today's port of Cádiz in Spain, which was "as far by water . . . as Jonah could possibly have sailed in those ancient days when the Atlantic was an almost unknown sea."

The Jonah that Mapple goes on to describe fits well with Calvin's assessment of someone "in a disturbed state of mind" (and perhaps it matches how you've imagined him as well):

> Miserable man! Oh most contemptible and worthy of all scorn; with slouched hat and guilty eye, skulking from his God; prowling among the shipping like a vile burglar hastening to cross the seas. . . . How plainly he's a fugitive! . . .
>
> At last, after much dodging search, he finds the Tarshish ship receiving the last items of her cargo; and as he steps on board to see its Captain in the cabin, all the sailors for the moment desist from hoisting in the goods, to mark the stranger's evil eye. Jonah sees this; but in vain he tries to look all ease and confidence.

The preacher imagines the other sailors guessing at this stranger's crime. Robbery? Murder? They don't suspect the crime of running from God. Jonah goes to the captain's quarters, finding him busy at his desk:

> "I seek a passage in the ship to Tarshish; how soon sail ye, sir?"
>
> Thus far the busy Captain had not looked up to Jonah . . . but no sooner does he hear that hollow voice, than he darts a scrutinizing glance. "We sail with the next coming tide," at last he slowly answered, still intently eyeing him.
>
> "No sooner, sir?"
>
> "Soon enough for any honest man that goes a passenger."

Ha! Jonah! That's another stab. But he swiftly calls away the Captain from that scent. "I'll sail with ye," he says. "The passage money, how much is that? I'll pay now."

The captain, like the crew, suspects Jonah of being a criminal. But he quickly ignores that impression when Jonah agrees to pay a sum that's three times the usual rate of passage—only confirming the captain's guess that Jonah is a fugitive.[2]

If Melville's imagined portrait here is anywhere close to reality, it's quite a step down for this esteemed prophet from Galilee.

WHAT GOD HURLS

The story of Jonah now enters its first extended scene. We're aboard that Tarshish-bound ship with the runaway prophet. Immediately God confirms just how impossible it is for anyone to flee the Lord's presence:

> But the LORD hurled a great wind upon the sea, and there was a mighty tempest on the sea, so that the ship threatened to break up. (1:4)

This story leaves no room for doubt about who's in control. The storm he sends is described first as a "great" wind (there's that Hebrew word *gadol* again). The God of all creation is very capable of brewing up a massive storm with the blink of an eye. (And as we see in the Gospels, he's also capable of calming that storm in an instant.)

In this story that features lean, straightforward phrasing, the attention given to the storm is remarkable: it's "a great wind upon the sea" and "a mighty tempest on the sea." This is no ordinary squall. Already the loss of ship and life seems imminent, though, as we'll see, the storm's worst is yet to come.

When we run from God, his response is more likely to be stormy and upsetting than quiet and subtle. He knows how to make us miserable. And it makes those around us miserable as well:

> Then the mariners were afraid, and each cried out to his god. And they hurled the cargo that was in the ship into the sea to lighten it for them. (1:5)

These are not queasy landlubbers, but hardy, seasoned "mariners" who know well the sea's stormy ways. If they're afraid, they have good reason to be. Jonah's actions have placed them in serious danger.

In their fear, they cry out each to his own god, knowing they're face-to-face with the powers of chaos. H. L. Ellison, in his commentary on Jonah, helps us understand their belief system:

> For the ancient Near East, the gods had created order by defeating the powers of chaos; but these had been tamed, not abolished, and so remained a constant threat. The embodiment of these lawless and chaotic forces was the sea, which men could not control or tame.[3]

Fearing this chaos, the sailors "hurled" their cargo into that untamed ocean, while God kept hurling the storm. In this contest, it isn't difficult to imagine who'll win.

THE DOWNWARD DRAG

Meanwhile, what about their passenger?

> But Jonah had gone down into the inner part of the ship and had lain down and was fast asleep. (1:5)

A shocker once again. Jonah's insensible withdrawal is not only astonishing and perplexing but even disgusting. He sinks lower in our esteem.

The wording of the story conveys well his descending spiral. Jonah had gone "down" to Joppa to find the ship, he went "down" into the ship's hold, and he lay "down" and now sleeps. In the sermon at New Bedford, Chaplain Mapple described Jonah's lowness this way: "A deep stupor steals over him, as over the man who bleeds to death, for conscience is the wound. . . . Jonah's prodigy of ponderous misery drags him drowning down to sleep."[4]

Flight from God always leads downward. It culminates not in the vivacious life we imagined but in what amounts only to stagnant sleep. It's why so many people seem to exist without ever really living. In fact, they *aren't* really living; they're only going through the motions—rarely if ever experiencing the internal *shalom* they were designed to enjoy from God, because they're running from him.

Running from God brings a cost not only to us but also to those around us. Think about this: there's another incident narrated in the Bible where a man of God is a passenger on a ship headed westward in the Mediterranean, with mostly pagans on board, and the ship is hit by a remarkably intense storm so severe that here again the ship's crew jettisons the cargo, and all hope of surviving dies away. But in this second story, found in Acts 27, what a difference we see in the behavior of the man of God on board.

That man was Paul, on a journey to Rome as a prisoner. He encourages the despairing crew, speaking boldly and convincingly of God's personal assurance to him that all of them will indeed come out alive. He steps into a leadership vacuum to direct the ship's officers and men, and ultimately helps save every life on board.

By contrast, Jonah's lethargic withdrawal from reality reminds me of the remarkable book *The Great Divorce,* where C. S. Lewis so vividly portrays the difference between people on their way to heaven and those on their way to hell. We see how those who flee from God become increasingly thin and insubstantial and see-through, while those who pursue him become progressively more real and intense and solid. Those running from God become less human the farther they run; those running toward him become more human the closer they get. The more human we are, the more we become what God wants us to become, and the better it is for those around us. The less human we are, the worse it is for those around us.

When I was a kid and traveled by airplane with my parents, I remember being mightily offended by the flight attendant explaining the safety regulations before our takeoff. As she described the oxygen masks and then added, "If you're traveling with small children, put the mask on your own face before putting one on the face of your child," I thought, *How mean! Good parents should care more about their child's breathing than their own.* Only later did I get it: parents who aren't breathing are of no use to their child.

Running from God keeps you from "breathing" and living the life he intends you to live. You thereby rob other people of the blessing God intends to give them through you, because you're less than you're meant to be—as Jonah's descending spiral vividly testifies.

This downward path that leads to death is typically slow and gradual, coming on more like the tides than a tidal wave. It's a numbing of our senses that happens slowly and subtly, like the experience of the frog in the heated water kettle. For Jonah, however, the pace of the downward spiral is accelerated, thanks to God.

"THAT WE MAY NOT PERISH"

The fugitive's sleep is interrupted:

> So the captain came and said to him, "What do you mean, you sleeper? Arise, call out to your god! Perhaps the god will give a thought to us, that we may not perish." (1:6)

If we as readers are amazed at Jonah's sleeping through the perfect storm, how much more astonished would this captain be, already soaked and battered from fighting the deafening reality of wind and waves. "You sleeper!" the captain calls him, and it isn't a compliment. All the other men have prayed as never before to their own gods, yet the storm only worsens. Jonah, the captain insists, needs to try praying as well.

As Jonah's groggy mind awakens to their turbulent, desperate reality, is he ashamed? Irritated? Frightened? Overwhelmed? Does he pray to his God, as the captain asked him to? We aren't told.

Jonah joins the sailors. By now they know that help from the gods is their only hope. But their help seems blocked. Someone's to blame for that—and no doubt the sailors share a common opinion about the culprit's identity. They know a way to flush him out:

> And they said to one another, "Come, let us cast lots, that we may know on whose account this evil has come upon us." (1:7)

Jonah is probably repelled by this whole business of lot-casting by worshipers of false gods. But how can he protest—he, the sleeper, a rebel runaway from the true God?

> So they cast lots, and the lot fell on Jonah. (1:7)

The truth of Proverbs 16:33 is confirmed: "The lot is cast into the lap, but its every decision is from the LORD."

PINNED DOWN

Calvin notes that these sailors would not be so quick to single out one man "if each had well considered what he deserved before God. When a calamity happens, it is the duty of every one to examine himself and his whole life before God; then everyone, from the first to the last, must confess that he bears a just judgment." These men seek one person to blame for the storm, Calvin says, "because they did not think that their own sins deserved so heavy a punishment."[5]

But however sinful these sailors may be, in this case God is pinning down Jonah, not them. The Creator and Sovereign of all things allowed this casting of lots by idol-worshipers to expose the shame and guilt of his own prophet.

With the culprit now duly exposed, we wouldn't be surprised if these storm-tossed, terrified, superstitious sailors throw Jonah overboard at this very moment, no questions asked. But there's more to these men than we might imagine—including no shortage of restraint and sensitivity.

> Then they said to him, "Tell us on whose account this evil has come upon us. What is your occupation? And where do you come from? What is your country? And of what people are you?" (1:8)

In the story, Jonah now speaks for the very first time as he answers their barrage of questions with a simple confession.

> And he said to them, "I am a Hebrew, and I fear the LORD, the God of heaven, who made the sea and the dry land." (1:9)

In this intense moment, the first thing Jonah confesses is his *nationality.* That's worth remembering as the story progresses.

The second thing he confesses is his fear of the true God, the creator of earth and ocean. In the chapel sermon in *Moby Dick,* Mapple says this answer "is forced from Jonah by the hard hand of God that is upon him."[6] But is Jonah being honest here? Or is he simply trying to claim innocence? Tellingly, Jonah's words bring a profound reaction from the sailors.

> Then the men were exceedingly afraid and said to him, "What is this that you have done!" For the men knew that he

was fleeing from the presence of the LORD, because he had told them. (1:10)

What have you done! the sailors shout. As H. L. Ellison points out, "It is an exclamation, not a question."[7] They see quite clearly what this guy has done, and it defies all sense and reason. They're horrified, "exceedingly afraid"—literally "terrified with a great (*gadol*) terror." With Jonah's answer, the truth pierces their hearts that the God their passenger has insulted is the creator of this very ocean (unlike their own gods), and the only controller of this chaos.

Only now are we told that Jonah had previously informed them of his intended flight from the Lord. Calvin states that this indicates how Jonah is not trying to evade blame here but only confirming it. He isn't hiding or holding back anything. But God's trap is still closing in on him.

GROWING FEAR, GROWING STORM

When Jonah confesses, "I *fear* the LORD, the God of heaven," he's at least beginning to do exactly that. And he's about to be given even more reason to fear God.

Then they said to him, "What shall we do to you, that the sea may quiet down for us?" For the sea grew more and more tempestuous. (1:11)

The sailors, and perhaps Jonah as well, may have thought that with the lots now cast and Jonah's guilt openly identified and confessed, the God-sent storm will start to diminish. But, no, it gets worse—"more and more tempestuous." Will it ever end? And if so, *how*?

Something must be done; something must be done *to Jonah*. What exactly? The sailors seem reluctant to act, and they instead ask Jonah's advice on how to deal with him.

> He said to them, "Pick me up and hurl me into the sea; then the sea will quiet down for you, for I know it is because of me that this great tempest has come upon you." (1:12)

His answer is another shocker: *Drown me.* But is it really so surprising? Is Jonah being heroic? Perhaps not so much. The ever-increasing storm—"this great [*gadol*] tempest"—is surely about to take *all* their lives as it finally destroys the ship. Jonah has enough restored clarity in his prophet's mind and spirit to know that the Lord his God, creator of the sea and dry land, has assuredly sent this storm *because of him* and will indeed calm that storm once he's thrown to the waves. That's the bottom line, and Jonah states it forthrightly to the sailors. "Jonah speaks here by the prophetic spirit; and he no doubt confirms," Calvin says, "that the God of Israel was the supreme and only King of heaven and earth."[8]

So Jonah's two choices are these: (a) death by drowning with all the ship's crew, or (b) death by drowning alone, with the sailors' lives spared. From a purely selfish standpoint, perhaps there was hardly a difference. Surrounded by these sailors, Jonah tells them that he chooses to die without them.

NO MORE OPTIONS

But they're still reluctant, still cautious and caring. "There was," Jerome H. Smith observes, "great humanity and tender feeling in these men."[9]

> Nevertheless, the men rowed hard to get back to dry land, but they could not, for the sea grew more and more tempestuous against them. (1:13)

Amazingly, they try to make for land, which surely has already proven impossible (or else it would have been the best and obvious solution long before). But the harder they try, the higher the waves mount, the fiercer the wind shrieks. The storm's unbelievable rage grows unbelievably worse.

Trapped as they are, this ship is like a shrunken world to them. There's no Tarshish anymore, no Joppa, no Nineveh, no Israel, no land at all—all of that is now out of reach, seemingly forever. There's only this fragile ship carrying living human beings, barely suspended over this gaping gray expanse of wet chaos and death.

Their ship can't last. The men have no other option than the one Jonah declared to them.

> Therefore they called out to the LORD, "O LORD, let us not perish for this man's life, and lay not on us innocent blood, for you, O LORD, have done as it pleased you." (1:14)

Three times in this verse, God's covenant name—*Yahweh*, the LORD—is used as he is entreated by these lifelong worshipers of false deities. They confess that this ever-magnifying tempest is fully his action and his sovereign right. And far from being contemptuous toward his prophet Jonah, they respect him—and value his life.

Do their words pierce the prophet's heart, while he's mere moments away from his own death? We don't know.

> So they picked up Jonah and hurled him into the sea, and the sea ceased from its raging. (1:15)

Their deed is done—and so is the storm. The Lord God extinguishes the tempest. The rage is spent, the sea surface goes suddenly calm. It's the most astounding thing these men have ever witnessed. They've been given the opportunity to clearly see the Lord God's power at work, and they respond as best they know.

> Then the men feared the LORD exceedingly, and they offered a sacrifice to the LORD and made vows. (1:16)

Literally, they "feared the LORD with great [*gadol*] fear."

All in all, the contrast in this scene between Jonah and the sailors could hardly be stronger. The proud "Hebrew" and self-proclaimed God-fearer has shown rash resistance to God's authority, character, and purposes. The pagan Gentiles, meanwhile, consistently demonstrate sensitivity to God's sovereignty and supremacy, as well as to the sanctity of human life.

MUGGED

Among the helpful lessons Jonah's story offers at this point is the obvious one: *you can't outrun God.* It's futile to try. It's impossible to outpace his pursuing affection.

C. S. Lewis tried. In his autobiographical work *Surprised by Joy*, he tells of his years spent as an atheist. "I had always wanted, above all things, not to be 'interfered with.' I had wanted (mad wish) 'to call my soul my own.'" But God interfered, as Lewis relates: "You must picture me alone in that room . . . night after night, feeling, whenever my mind lifted even for a second from my work, the steady, unrelenting approach of Him whom I so earnestly desired not to meet."[10]

Francis Thompson also tried to run, as he tells in his poem "The Hound of Heaven," beginning with these famous lines:

> I fled Him, down the nights and down the days;
> I fled Him, down the arches of the years;
> I fled Him, down the labyrinthine ways
> Of my own mind; and in the mist of tears
> I hid from Him, and under running laughter.

Thompson fled, but God, hounding him from heaven, gave "long pursuit" with "strong Feet that followed, followed after," and with "a Voice above their beat."[11] God's love has a mugging nature to it. We can run, but we can't hide.

MASSIVE MERCY

Another lesson: *God's mercy is massive.* This storm tells us that God spares no expense in going after those who run away.

God could easily have raised up someone else to do the work Jonah refused. It's not like the Lord's hands were tied or that after sending the storm he kept his fingers crossed, hoping his unruly servant would at last respond. God is never in such weakness. He's always in the position of authority and control, whether or not we realize it.

The supreme example of this massive mercy is Jesus. The incarnation of Christ tells us most emphatically how God spares nothing in going after those who run away. God's becoming man is anything but a quiet and subtle response from God to our running from him. It's a huge and loud statement. It shouts to us that God confronts human flight in the most outspoken, powerful way.

Of all the world's religions, only in Christianity does God become one of his creatures. *God* becoming *human?* That's massive, deafening—anything but subtle. Jesus is really God's "great wind," his "mighty tempest" in response to human running and rebellion. *Jesus is the storm.* Jesus is God's gracious intervention for those who are enslaved to themselves. He comes loudly, not subtly, with an aggressive affection to pursue fugitives like you and me.

INTERVENTION, NOT PUNISHMENT

When we first read this part of the story, we typically assume the storm is Jonah's punishment from God for his disobedience. But the storm isn't punishment; it's an intervention, brought on by God's affection rather than his anger.

Interventions are for those who are in great trouble and don't realize it—for those who are self-destructing yet living in denial. Jonah doesn't recognize the great trouble he's in. With his very life imperiled, he sleeps. But Jonah's greatest danger isn't physical but spiritual. He's not just running from God physically; he's fleeing spiritually.

Would it have been better for Jonah if God had left him alone? No, it would have been far worse. It was an act of mercy for God to send the storm. As C. S. Lewis reminded us in *Surprised by Joy,* "The hardness of God is kinder than the softness of men, and His compulsion is our liberation."[12]

Jonah desperately *needs* an intervention. This storm was God-sent to liberate Jonah from *Jonah.* It was God's way of loosing Jonah's chains of self-dependence. Jonah thought that running from God would make him free. Instead it made him a slave. We can experience true life and freedom only when we come to realize that God is God and we are not—something Jonah was profoundly resisting.

Submitting self to God is the only real freedom—because the deepest slavery is self-dependence, self-reliance. When you live your life believing that everything (family, finances, relationships, career) depends primarily on *you,* you're enslaved to your strengths and weaknesses. You're trying to be your own savior. Freedom comes when we start trusting in God's abilities and wisdom instead of our own. Real life begins when we transfer our trust from our own efforts to the efforts of Christ.

FALLEN CHAINS

This part of Jonah's story points to the good news that God is the freer of slaves. This story *shows* us what Jesus *tells* us at the beginning of his ministry: "The Spirit of the Lord is upon me, because he has anointed me to proclaim good news to the poor. He has sent me to proclaim liberty to the captives and recovering of sight to the blind, to set at liberty those who are oppressed" (Luke 4:18).

Everything Jesus said he came to do was what the storm came to do for Jonah. The storm was good news to Jonah, who'd become spiritually impoverished; it was there to open his blind eyes and to liberate him from self-oppression. And just as the storm was sent to release Jonah, so Jesus sets free self-enslaved captives like you and me. I doubt anyone has captured this truth better than Charles Wesley in his remarkable hymn *And Can It Be That I Should Gain?* Here he describes his own conversion—and essentially that of every sinner:

> Long my imprisoned spirit lay
> fast-bound in sin and nature's night.
> Thine eye diffused a quickening ray,
> I woke; the dungeon flamed with light.
> My chains fell off, my heart was free,
> I rose, went forth, and followed Thee.[13]

That's the freedom offered to all and made available to all by God's relentless pursuit through the storm of Jesus Christ.

TWO WAYS OF RUNNING

When you understand that it was God's affection for Jonah that sent the intervening storm—and that it's God's affection for you and me that sent an intervening Savior—it begs the question: Why run? God's intervention comes to two different kinds of people, because, as Jonah's story shows, there are two ways of running from God. All of us fall into one of the two categories.

One way of running is probably more obvious to you than the other. It's represented by the pagan sailors, especially as Jonah would perceive them. These mariners obviously were worshipers of false gods, and therefore unrighteous. They're like the people Paul speaks about in Romans 1. People like this are ungodly and sensual. They live according to the world's standards, usually without apology. They're so disconnected from God's ways that they live however they want. This is the condition of those outside the church, those who don't know God. They're like the prodigal son in the story Jesus told, the younger brother who runs off and gives himself to immoral, riotous living.

But there's also a not-so-obvious way of running from God, and the fact that it's less clear is perhaps a big part of why we're so surprised by Jonah's behavior. Jonah was one of the good guys. He cared about God's law and God's chosen people. He was moral and religious—like the older brother in Jesus' story of the prodigal son. If Jonah were here today, he wouldn't be the long-haired, tattooed indie rocker, but the clean-cut prep conservative. He sounds like a lot of people in the church, doesn't he? But despite his pedigree and profile, *Jonah's still running from God*. He's no better off than the sailors. His morality and correct religion have brought him no closer to God than the sailors' worldliness and false religion.

TWO PURSUITS OF SALVATION

These two types of runners try to save themselves in two different ways. Immoral people try to save themselves through licentious living—liberally and lawlessly. Moral people try to save themselves through legalistic living. The immoral try to save themselves by breaking the law; the moral try to save themselves by keeping it. But neither way is strong enough to save anybody.

Only the gospel can save. In *The Reason for God,* Tim Keller writes this:

> If you're avoiding sin and living morally so that God will have to bless you and save you, then you may be looking to Jesus as a teacher, model, and helper, but ironically you are avoiding him as Savior. You are trusting in your own goodness rather than in Jesus for your standing with God.[14]

This is self-reliance rearing its ugly head. Self-reliance is the natural tendency of every human heart, and it festers in the heart of the Christian as much as in the heart of the non-Christian—just in a different way.

Only the gospel can truly save you. The gospel doesn't make bad people good; *it makes dead people alive.* That's the difference between the gospel of Jesus Christ and every other world religion. All the others exhort their followers to save themselves by being good, by conforming their lives to whatever their worshiped deity is. But the gospel is God's acceptance of us based on what *Christ* has done, not on what we can do.

Grace can be defined as *unconditional acceptance granted to an undeserving person by an unobligated giver.* Only God offers this kind of total acceptance without condition. Moralistic religion wrongly teaches us to say, "I obey, therefore, God must accept me." The gospel rightly teaches us to say, "When I trust in Jesus, God accepts me; therefore I obey."

Isn't it interesting how, in the New Testament, it's the immoral who "get" the gospel before the moral do? It's the irreligious, not the religious, who embrace it first. It's the prostitute, not the Pharisee; the unrighteous younger brother, not the self-righteous older brother. That's why Jesus said, "I came not to call the righteous, but sinners" (Mark 2:17). He wasn't saying there are those who are righteous enough that they don't need salvation. He was saying, "I came to save those who know they're unrighteous." Those who think that their righteousness—their rightness—is capable of earning God's favor will never listen to Jesus, because they don't see their desperation. They don't realize they're running from God.

Even when we know God, we still tend to run from him in one of these two ways. You're facing a difficult season in life—things aren't going well, for whatever reason—and either you say, "Forget it," and just let yourself go (trying to rescue yourself by being bad), or you say, "I've got to pull myself together," and you strive to regain control (trying to rescue yourself by being good). Either way, you're looking to yourself—not Christ—for rescue.

But God's grace is so massive that it tracks down both types of runners—the lawbreakers and the lawkeepers, the moral and the immoral, the good and the bad. The story of Jonah proves that. Whenever we try running from God, he's committed to making our lives miserable—for our sakes. And so often, he'll use some kind of storm to do it, not to punish but to mercifully intervene.

OUR OWN STORMS

Until we see God-sent storms as interventions and not punishments, we'll never get better; we'll only get bitter. Some difficult circumstances you're facing right now may well be a God-sent storm of mercy intended to be his intervention in your life.

You're in danger, and either you don't realize it or you're living in denial. How are you responding?

You may feel frustrated, bitter, angry. You could be angry with yourself because you want to control things better than you are. Or you're angry with God, intuitively if not consciously. Or perhaps, like the sailors, you're facing an affliction that's someone else's fault, and you're angry at that person. Whatever the case, the question is: Are you crying out to God for help and rescue?

Psalm 107 is a great help in this way—a great comfort, a great pillow on which to rest our weary heads. This psalm shows two types of people. There are those who suffer because they've dug themselves into a hole and those who suffer because they fell into a hole dug by others, the result of someone else's sin. But the common refrain for both types of people is this: "They cried to the LORD in their trouble."

Ultimately it doesn't matter whether your affliction is your fault or someone else's. You need not blame others or live under the guilt of self-blame. The real question is: Are you responding by crying to the Lord for deliverance?

When difficulty comes, it's an opportunity to find out something about ourselves: did we enter into a relationship with God so he could serve us or so we could serve him? A friend of mine recently wrote these words:

> If we are really seeking to serve God, we will be willing to wait on Him through the darkness, so that when it lifts, He will have turned a lump of coal into a shining diamond, so that we will have a peace, an unflappability, and a strength that we did

not have before and would not have had if we had not gone through the darkness.

We need to be able to truthfully say, "God plus nothing equals everything; everything minus God equals nothing." We need to be able to say from our hearts, "I'm with God because he's God, and not because he can do for me the things I want him to do." We need to be able to say and mean, "I don't need to get anything out of my relationship with God right now." Instead of being affected by our gloomy circumstances, we need to be affected by what Jesus gloriously did for us on the cross.

It's only then that you'll see these storms of affliction as God-sent, merciful intrusions in your life, designed to wake you up, unlock your chains, and free you to become the person God wants you to become.

Scene 2:

IN A GREAT FISH

Let us then with confidence draw near to the throne of grace,
that we may receive mercy and find grace to help in time of need.
HEBREWS 4:16

✜

Try running from God, and there's no telling where you'll
end up.

As he dashed to Joppa to find an outbound ship,
Jonah certainly never dreamed he'd soon be sinking beneath the
Mediterranean's storm waves. His downward progression to
this lowest of lows has been staggeringly fast. For most who run
from God, the plunge is slower. That's why I tell young men that
the adultery that destroys marriage at age forty gets started with
wandering eyes at age twenty.

A LOVELY TURMOIL

"And now behold Jonah," proclaims Mapple the preacher in
Moby Dick, "taken up as an anchor and dropped into the sea."

The setting for Mapple's sermon, you may recall, was a
seamen's chapel in New Bedford, Massachusetts, one of the
nineteenth-century's greatest whaling ports. During the time
when Herman Melville was writing *Moby Dick* and getting it

published, one of the youngsters roaming the teeming streets and wharves of New Bedford was a boy named Albert Ryder. He would grow up to become "one of America's greatest, most enigmatic artists"[1] and "one of the greatest visionary painters of all time."[2] Reflecting his New Bedford upbringing, many of his works would feature deep-colored, motion-filled seascapes, especially in a haunting portrait showing Jonah just after he was thrown overboard. It's a fascinating, unforgettable image that endures as one of Ryder's most famous works.

Ryder may well have identified personally with Jonah, particularly as a castaway and a loner. He tended to live reclusively, despite the increasing acclaim he achieved over his lifetime. Revered for his brooding, lyrical, dreamlike paintings, and admired by other artists for his complete devotion to his work, he also became known for his eccentric and slovenly ways—perhaps not unlike the sleeping Jonah in the Tarshish-bound ship.

In later years Ryder turned increasingly to biblical subjects and the theme of good versus evil. He seemed to be "asserting his faith against the challenge of Darwinism."[3] He may have felt a deeply religious kinship with Jonah; the most prominent biography of the artist states that "Ryder's adult life, as reflected in his letters and reports by his friends, was highly moral and, in the larger sense, committed to spiritual values, with God playing a prominent role in his thoughts and feelings."[4] That description also fits Jonah, especially in how the prophet seemed to view himself, as we'll see later in his story.

Ryder's rendition of Jonah[5] is described by the painter's first biographer as something "which has no real counterpart in the art of any time or place . . . a picture that belongs with the greatest of those that have been inspired by Scripture."[6] The painting is dominated by frothing, violent waves, murky and churning in a great clockwise swirl, perhaps capturing in some way the awful view they must have presented to Jonah himself. While Ryder was working on this painting, he wrote in a letter, "I am in ecstasies over my Jonah; such a lovely turmoil of boiling water and everything." Jonah, thrown into it, would doubtless have testified to the turmoil without seeing much loveliness.

In the center of these convulsive waves in Ryder's painting we see the ship, open and unmasted, crowded with the shadowy figures of the sailors who seem to cower beneath the storm's assault. The vessel itself is weirdly bent, another sign of the storm's power.

In the image's foreground—closest to us, so we easily identify with him—is the frail man Jonah up to his neck in the sea. His arms are raised, caught in mid-flail. He faces us, his back to the ship. His mouth is open, surely about to gulp in the waters that will drown him. But behind him, off to one side, a sea creature with bulging eyes approaches, gliding through the stormy surface. It's as big as the ship.

And still further behind Jonah, overarching all this scene, is the painting's most startling image. The far horizon, in great contrast to the sea's churning darkness, is spanned by winglike clouds in white and gold. In their center we see someone we know at once is a representation of God. In his right palm rests an orb, while his extended left hand conveys a gesture of blessing, thumb and two fingers raised. His golden-bearded head bends attentively forward. His face is watchful but unworried. We sense immediately his calm sovereignty and wisely gracious intention. It's all so starkly counter to what we see and feel happening in the ocean swells around Jonah.

With the prophet dropped into the stormy sea like a cast anchor—what is it that the sovereign, gracious, all-wise God has planned for him?

DESPERATION

What's next in Jonah's story is by far our biggest shock yet, although, as an amazed Calvin noted, the event is recorded "as though it were an ordinary thing":[7]

> And the LORD appointed a great fish to swallow up Jonah. And Jonah was in the belly of the fish three days and three nights. (1:17)

This sea creature—this great (*gadol*) fish—"is in exactly the right place at the right time by God's command, in order to swallow Jonah and enclose him safely."[8] To be sustained for so long in such a place is an unquestionable miracle—totally God-appointed.

What was it like for Jonah inside there? Mostly it's unimaginable; what we can envision, realistically, is terrifying and repulsive, to say the least. But giving us an insider's take on "How to Survive Three Days in a Fish's Belly" is not where this story's headed. The focus isn't Jonah and the fish but *Jonah and God*. It isn't about mere physical survival, but spiritual revival. So we read:

> Then Jonah prayed to the LORD his God from the belly of the fish. (2:1)

Of all the places mentioned in the Bible where people prayed, this has to be the most unusual. Jonah is desperate. And like most desperate people, he turns to God.

In desperation, he prays—like David: "*This poor man cried,* and the LORD heard him and saved him out of all his troubles" (Ps. 34:6).

In desperation, he prays—like Hannah: "*She was deeply distressed* and prayed to the LORD and wept bitterly" (1 Sam. 1:10).

In desperation, he prays—like Jeremiah: "Water closed over my head; I said, '*I am lost.*' I called on your name, O LORD, from the depths of the pit; you heard my plea, 'Do not close your ear to *my cry for help!*'" (Lam. 3:54–56).

In desperation, he prays—like Jesus, as he also faced three days and three nights in the darkest of places: "And *being in an agony* he prayed more earnestly; and his sweat became like great drops of blood falling down to the ground" (Luke 22:44).

In desperation, Jonah prays—exactly as God wants us all to do in such times: "Is anyone among you suffering? *Let him pray*" (James 5:13).

LIKE HELL

Jonah's prayer is written down for us as a psalm, some thirty brief lines of poetry. It's full of phrases and images that we find also throughout the book of Psalms, especially in the psalms written by David. We see that Jonah knows God's written word well and can return to it and embrace it, even after he's guilty of blatantly disobeying God's spoken word.

What Jonah's psalm declares most emphatically is this: *God hears my prayer!* Five times Jonah mentions the extreme anguish that prompted him to pray; then each time he comes back to trusting awareness of an amazing fact he just can't seem to get over: *God has heard me and is rescuing me!* We discover a two-part rhythm in his psalm, like the surf—swelling then receding, swelling then receding, again and again: My agony, *God's response*. . . . My agony, *God's response*. . . . Notice the pattern first in these opening lines:

> I called out to the LORD, out of my distress,
>> and he answered me;
> out of the belly of Sheol I cried,
>> and you heard my voice. (2:2)

Sheol, a Hebrew word that can mean "hell," gives us a good clue as to how Jonah is sensing and experiencing all this.

The psalm then dwells longer on his distress before bringing another triumphant expression of faith in God's response:

> For you cast me into the deep,
>> into the heart of the seas,
>> and the flood surrounded me;
> all your waves and your billows
>> passed over me.
> Then I said, "I am driven away
>> from your sight;
> yet I shall again look
>> upon your holy temple." (2:3–4)

This last statement about looking upon God's temple expresses Jonah's hope not only of deliverance but also of his restoration to the faith of God's people. This assurance came only after he'd first lost hope of ever connecting personally with God again. He felt "driven away" from God's sight. How many of us have felt that same severance from God in our own times of trouble? David certainly felt it, in this passage that Jonah must have recalled:

> I had said in my alarm,
>   "I am cut off from your sight."
> But you heard the voice of my pleas for mercy
>   when I cried to you for help. (Ps. 31:22)

Equally significant here is how Jonah says it was *God,* not the sailors, who cast him into the deep. This represents, as Wayne Grudem points out, "a remarkable illustration of God's concurrence in human activity":

> The providential direction of God did not force the sailors to do something against their will, nor were they conscious of any divine influence on them—indeed, they cried to the Lord for forgiveness as they threw Jonah overboard (Jonah 1:14). What Scripture reveals to us, and what Jonah himself realized, was that God was bringing about his plan through the willing choices of real human beings who were morally responsible for their actions. In a way not understood by us and not revealed to us, God *caused* them to make a *willing choice* to do what they did.[9]

Jonah's world may be collapsing into unimaginable calamity, but still he's enabled to see that God is in control.

PASSING AWAY

Next in Jonah's psalm comes another extended look at his agony—more graphic this time—with the rhythm returning again to articulate faith in his deliverance.

The waters closed in over me to take my life;
    the deep surrounded me;
weeds were wrapped about my head
    at the roots of the mountains.
I went down to the land
    whose bars closed upon me forever;
yet you brought up my life from the pit,
    O LORD my God. (2:5–6)

In his trauma, enshrouded with seaweed, Jonah feels himself descending to an underworld prison, the place of death and condemnation. But God, astoundingly, is lifting him out. It's as if this tormented man, in his awful, God-enforced darkness, can hear a future voice coming to him across the centuries from the Son of Man: "Even the hairs of your head are all numbered. *Fear not*" (Matt. 10:30–31).

Then comes a short summary of Jonah's situation, still in the same two-part pattern:

When my life was fainting away,
    I remembered the LORD,
and my prayer came to you,
    into your holy temple. (2:7)

His prayer springs from the panic of sensing his life giving out—something David had once felt inwardly, as expressed in Psalm 61:2: "From the end of the earth I call to you when my heart is faint."

We might be tempted to rush through this prayer of Jonah's while thinking he's only repeating stock Scripture phrases out of religious habit. We might even fail to see much genuineness of emotion here, perhaps forgetting that we who've never been detained for days inside a sea monster's bowels shouldn't be too hasty in judging someone who has.

We may also tend to overlook how, in our own times of severe distress, simple phrases from the Psalms can carry a world of weight and significance while we long to be delivered. Each of our greatest afflictions is terrible in its own way, but surely Jonah's was nothing less than the very worst any of us has ever encountered.

INNUMERABLE DEATHS

Calvin, with his usual insight and sympathy, probes deeply into the prophet's inner condition here, while adding, "It is certain that no one of us can comprehend, much less convey in words, what must have come into the mind of Jonah during these three days." Jonah may recognize that he's "unworthy of undergoing a common or an ordinary punishment"; he is instead "exiled, as it were, from the world, so as to be deprived of light and air." During those dark endless hours in such a ghastly prison, "he must have suffered a continual execution"; he would conclude that God, instead of killing him off at once, has decided to expose him "to innumerable deaths." Entrapped so severely by his Creator and Lord, he "languished in continual torments" and "continually boiled with grief."[10] No wonder Jonah speaks of the fish's belly as "the belly of Sheol."

But the Lord—extending a mercy that is unspeakably amazing—enables Jonah to see his situation with more clarity. The fish's belly was not Jonah's prison or death chamber, but only a temporary hospital for his soul and a protection for his body from the ocean depths. It's *good* for Jonah to be here. God ensures that his unworthy servant is made fully aware of this undeserved deliverance.

Jonah at last is thinking more clearly, after all his absurd maneuvering to flee God's assignment and God's presence. He's reconnecting with some essentials of spiritual life, embracing them more deeply than ever.

Jonah felt doomed to certain death, yet he's miraculously spared. While staring oblivion in the face, the prophet who had rushed to leave God behind now found himself crying out in terror, "I am driven away from your sight" (2:4). God has heard his cry, and Jonah hears and believes the promise of a future in the Lord's presence.

We can safely assume that these psalm-words reflect the most memorable thoughts and feelings of Jonah's mind and heart during this time, perhaps interspersed with his drifting in and out of consciousness while undergoing such a trauma. God has closed him in as tightly as possible; every human comfort and distraction might just as well be a universe away. Shut in like this to nothingness, Jonah reconnects with the God he spurned.

Hawaiian artist Dennis McGeary depicts Jonah's condition well in a 2001 abstract painting done entirely in black, white, and gray.[11] A mass of contoured lines takes up nearly all the painting, suggesting simultaneously both the interior massiveness of a whale-like creature and the swirling waves of the storm. Almost hidden in the center, a few of the lines are bent up, sail-like—the tiny ship in the storm. Along the uprising lines on a lower side we see a man falling, his hands raised uselessly as he descends where he does not wish to go—Jonah cast overboard. Finally, set off in an undersized black square in the opposite corner, is the small, hunkered form of the swallowed prophet, brooding over what has happened to him. How he must wonder at God's design in all this!

EVEN HERE

Jonah's prayerful words from inside the fish draw so deeply from the treasury of David's devotion that we can easily begin to link the two men. And this connection with David serves to link Jonah also with the Son of David, Jesus—and ultimately with all the people of God.

In profound ways, Jonah experienced *literally* the kinds of trials that David often expresses metaphorically. We see it in such emotion-filled passages from David as these:

> The cords of death encompassed me;
> > the torrents of destruction assailed me;
> the cords of Sheol entangled me;
> > the snares of death confronted me.
> In my distress I called upon the LORD;
> > to my God I cried for help.
> From his temple he heard my voice,
> > and my cry to him reached his ears. (Ps. 18:4–6)

> Save me, O God!
> > For the waters have come up to my neck. . . .
> I have come into deep waters,
> > and the flood sweeps over me. . . .
> Let me be delivered . . . from the deep waters.
> Let not the flood sweep over me,
> > or the deep swallow me up,
> > or the pit close its mouth over me. (Ps. 69:1–2, 14–15)

> For great is your steadfast love toward me;
> > you have delivered my soul from the depths of Sheol.
> > (Ps. 86:13)

David was never inside a fish, but he knew all too often the bitter heaviness of affliction. We see his typical response to such trial—and the example that Jonah followed—in 1 Samuel 30:6: *"David was greatly distressed,* for the people spoke of stoning him. . . . But *David strengthened himself in the* LORD *his God."*

David was doing what Israel's patriarchs had done long before him. When *"Jacob was greatly afraid and distressed,"* he prayed to the Lord, "Deliver me" (Gen. 32:7–11), and that very night he encountered God as never before.

Jonah, too, lets his unbearable distress direct him to the only true source of lasting help and deliverance. And since Jonah brought this suffering upon himself—yet rediscovers God in those dark consequences—he can even be seen as a fulfillment of David's sweeping acknowledgment of the Lord's omnipresence in Psalm 139:

> If I make my bed in Sheol, you are there! . . .
> If I . . .
>> dwell in the uttermost parts of the sea,
>> even there your hand shall lead me,
>> and your right hand shall hold me. (Ps. 139:8–10)

Even in Sheol, even in the uttermost parts of the sea, God's hand has tightened its hold on his unruly prophet.

IN CHARGE OF SALVATION

As Jonah's psalm concludes, we come to its most momentous lines. The prayer breaks out of the previous pattern, as Jonah contrasts others with himself.

> Those who pay regard to vain idols
>   forsake their hope of steadfast love.
> But I with the voice of thanksgiving
>   will sacrifice to you;
> what I have vowed I will pay.
>   Salvation belongs to the LORD! (2:8–9)

The "steadfast love" he speaks of is the Hebrew *hesed*, the ancient covenant term for God's unfailing mercy and lovingkindness—the very thing Jonah is now experiencing so overwhelmingly, so undeservingly. Jonah rightly observes that this love is something idolaters have no reason to expect from God. "But as for me," Jonah is saying, "I'll always be thankful for it, and respond appropriately."

In Jonah's words about idols, he again repeats the language of David, who said, "I hate *those who pay regard to worthless idols,* but I trust in the LORD" (Ps. 31:6). When Jonah speaks of these respecters of idols, is he thinking in general terms, since the whole world is filled with multitudes who worship false gods? Or does he have in mind some people in particular, like those superstitious sailors back on the ship?

Jonah ends his psalm with a simple statement packed with meaning: *"Salvation belongs to the LORD!"* "This is at once confession and praise," one commentary says; it's the sum of Jonah's song, and "the outcome of all he has passed through. Deliverance in its fullest sense is already his in faith and confident anticipation."[12] It's also an exact restatement of David's words, this time in Psalm 3:8, the very first psalm attributed to David.

A century and a half ago, Charles Spurgeon used a sermon

to explore the fullness of this declaration from Jonah. Salvation is "entirely of God," Spurgeon explained at length; it is God-sourced in its planning, in its execution, and in its application; it's also from God in how it's sustained in the human heart, and in how it's ultimately perfected in our eternal state.[13] *Salvation belongs to the Lord.*

In the generations that followed Jonah's time, God would speak through other prophets to reinforce Jonah's statement: "I am the LORD . . . *besides me there is no savior"* (Hos. 13:4; Isa. 43:11). Seven centuries later, this truth would form a backdrop for words Jesus spoke to a Samaritan woman: "Salvation is from the Jews" (John 4:22).

Jonah, in this final utterance of his psalm, is getting down to the most fundamental fact about restoring humanity's wholeness. Douglas Stuart in his commentary says that "there can be little doubt that this final declaration means . . . that salvation belongs to Yahweh in contrast to belonging to any other god, or coming from any other source." Inherent in Jonah's words, Stuart adds, is the connotation "that Yahweh is in charge of salvation, i.e., that he decides whom he will save and how. Salvation is his area of authority. In it, he alone makes the decisions."[14] This is a crucial point to remember as Jonah's story continues.

MISSING SOMETHING

We're likely to remember something else as well. Although Jonah's prayer displays "overtones of deep, emotional gratitude, of heartfelt thanks for deliverance, housed in the form Israelites knew so well to be employed by people joyously grateful for their own escape from danger," as Stuart summarizes it,[15] it's also missing something. And the omission looms large. There's no confession here of Jonah's sin—no acknowledgment of his stupidity and shamefulness in trying to shake off God in the first place.

Why is there no admission of his wrongdoing? Did Jonah actually confess it, yet it's something the story doesn't include, for whatever reason? Or was Jonah not really fully repentant? That's a question we'll come back to. For now at least, it appears that if anybody's going to be doing any repentance in this story, it won't be Jonah.

UP AND OUT

In full complement to the God-exalting tone of Jonah's psalm of thanksgiving, the next event in the story is another miracle of deliverance.

> And the LORD spoke to the fish, and it vomited Jonah out upon the dry land. (2:10)

In another wild display of God's grace and sovereignty, Jonah is getting a new beginning. The dark ordeal is over. But by God's providential design, Jonah's experience within the great fish represents something much bigger than he can realize. Jesus made that clear:

> For just as Jonah was three days and three nights in the belly of the great fish, so will the Son of Man be three days and three nights in the heart of the earth. (Matt. 12:40)

Both in Jonah and in the New Testament, "three days and

three nights" reflects an idiom from Hebrew culture, which counted any portion of a day as a full day. Jonah may have been inside the fish for about the same length of time as Jesus was buried "in the heart of the earth"—for an evening, and all the next day, then a few hours of the next.

Jonah's foreshadowing of the burial and resurrection of Jesus was so strong that Paul would declare how Jesus "was buried" and "was raised on the third day *in accordance with the Scriptures*" (1 Cor. 15:4). In accordance with *which* Scriptures? Only twice in the Old Testament is this three-day element prophesied—here in Jonah's story, and, less clearly, in Hosea, which was written just a generation after Jonah's time of ministry. In the Hosea passage, God's people say collectively, "*On the third day he will raise us up,* that we may live before him" (6:2). Taking together Hosea's prophecy along with the statement of Jesus, we again see the significance of Jonah's life intertwined not only with Christ's, but also with our own.

In a deep and mysterious way, Jonah, and Jesus in his humanity, and all the saints of God share an identity in the prophet's dark-depths entombment followed by expulsive release.

ALL ABOUT JESUS

We can thus imagine how Jesus—on the afternoon after his resurrection, when he walked and talked with two disciples on the road to Emmaus—would cite Jonah's story while he "interpreted to them in all the Scriptures the things concerning himself" (Luke 24:27). Later that night, when Jesus met with a larger group of disciples, he would likely refer to Jonah once more as "he opened their minds to understand the Scriptures" and declared to them "that everything written *about me* in the Law of Moses and the Prophets and the Psalms must be fulfilled" (24:44–45).

Jonah's story, he would say, is *about me.*

When Jonah was feeling death's approach in the depths of the sea, he had evidenced a typically limited Old Testament understanding of the afterlife when he instinctively spoke of sinking into Sheol and "the land whose bars closed upon me." But we know better! For "our Savior Christ Jesus" not only "abolished death" but also "brought *life and immortality to light* through the gospel" (2 Tim. 1:10). Christ's resurrection made clear forever our true and thrilling hope of eternal life, which is ours for the taking, all by faith. And in his mysterious and ever-surprising graciousness, the Lord has used the punishing ordeal of a rebel prophet to help make that point.

Jonah's experiences have become something altogether greater than he or anyone else could ever imagine. And now that he's freed from that fish . . . will Jonah's story finally settle down into something more even-keeled and predictable?

PART TWO

HEARTS EXPOSED

A New Beginning
AGAIN, GOD CALLS

*"You shall love the Lord your God with all your heart and with all
your soul and with all your mind and with all your strength."* . . .
"You shall love your neighbor as yourself."
There is no other commandment greater than these.

JESUS, IN MARK 12:30–31

Upchucked from a fish's throat and thrown onto dry
land—it all seems to indicate God's "sense of fun," one
commentary says—"depositing Jonah in this undigni-
fied fashion to clean himself up and start again."[1] It was indeed
a new start.

REACHING

Over the centuries, artistic representations of Jonah emerging
from the fish often give the impression that this guy has indeed
experienced something profound. We sense (and hope) that
he's now a changed man, ready for what's next. A case in point
is a much admired Italian Renaissance sculpture in marble by
Raphael and Lorenzetto; it shows a youthful, lean, energetic
figure with a face of serene determination.[2]

More recently, an eye-catching contemporary sculpture by
Phillip Ratner shows the great sea creature bursting straight up

through the water's surface, gigantic mouth opened wide. From it a slender Jonah is being ejected, with his face fixed upward. The sculpture's most memorable feature is Jonah's elongated arms reaching upward and Godward.[3]

This is a common motif in paintings of the emergent Jonah[4]— his arms upraised, as if in joy, relief, praise, prayer—or just to brace himself for landfall. In a work by Dutch painter Pieter Lastman in the 1600s, Jonah's entire body is midair between the giant fish's mouth and a rocky shore, and we can even see the wet spray of the fish's belch blast. Jonah's eyes are wide, and his lifted arms and straining legs are heavily muscled.

By contrast, in the Frenchman James Tissot's rendering in the 1800s, Jonah's frame is thin, almost gaunt; he wears a few flimsy, ragged remnants of his former attire as he wades ashore. With a tightened brow he casts a look over his shoulder at the tailfins of the fish diving away behind him. Here again, he holds up his arms before him, with the fingers almost touching.

In a stark 1975 painting by Salvador Dali of Spain, the naked prophet's limbs are all straight-locked as he leaps from the giant arc of the fish's mouth; the arms again stretch forward and up.

In a 2002 painting by Filipino-American artist Wayne Horte, Jonah's arms are raised with palms forward, fingers bent back. There are splotches of deep red (blood?) on his palms, his face, and elsewhere. His face is square and strong, his mouth is open, and we can almost hear a bold utterance ringing out from his throat.

What would Jonah be saying at this point? What is he feeling, thinking, planning, now that he's back in the land of the living? He tried to run from his Lord and Master, a course of action so wrong that God stopped him by sending the most intense storm the prophet had ever seen or heard of. Jonah may feel he's now worthy of being treated no better than a second-class member of God's people. Still, he must wonder: doesn't his miraculous deliverance mean that God has further plans for his prophet—not for evil, but to give him a future and a hope?

The tone we heard in Jonah's fish-belly psalm is like the symbolism we see in the upraised arms in all those paintings and sculptures. It's easy to feel confident that Jonah is now far more tuned into God than when this story began.

GRACE FOR RUNNERS FROM GOD

Without delay, the story brings us to Jonah's next divine encounter.

> Then the word of the LORD came to Jonah the second time, saying, "Arise, go to Nineveh, that great city, and call out against it the message that I tell you." (3:1–2)

In light of Jonah's earlier disobedience, what could possibly be more stunning to him—or more humbling—than to be so promptly recommissioned with his earlier assignment? And what could possibly be more gracious of God than to offer him this second chance? After all, it wasn't guaranteed. As H. L. Ellison cautions, we should not so easily "take the 'second time' for granted, as we are all too ready to do. There are many examples in the Scriptures of no second chance."[5]

But Jonah gets one. It's as if nothing has changed since God first called him to Nineveh. It's as if the holy and righteous God is choosing to forget Jonah's sin of disobedience and has hurled that sin into the sea depths (where no fish can ever swallow it, to vomit it up later). It's as if God has carried away that sin as far as the east is from the west.[6] God responds to great sin with great mercy!

We may still be bothered that Jonah hasn't acknowledged any wrongdoing, but God seems to have totally and unequivocally forgiven his rebel-hearted servant. For runners from God, there truly is such a thing as amazing grace.

When those who've fled from him are finally turned around, God always welcomes them back. The cross is God's greatest statement of that. He always welcomes—with open arms—those who realize that their only hope is to turn from themselves and race toward him.

FIXED BY GOD

As Jonah hears *for the second time* this personal calling to Nineveh, he recognizes that God is dead serious about his plans for that city. When a divine message is doubled, as Joseph knew when he interpreted Pharaoh's dreams, it "means that the thing is fixed by God, and God will shortly bring it about" (Gen. 41:32). God is resolute about giving Nineveh his message. Nothing will stop him.

As the Lord recommissions Jonah, he again reminds him that Nineveh is "great" (*gadol*). Along with the reissued command to "call out against it," God promises to give Jonah the specific words—"the message that I tell you." After feeling so cut off from God before, Jonah must be ecstatic to hear God speaking to him again—and promising to tell him more. Without delay, Jonah responds.

> So Jonah arose and went to Nineveh, according to the word
> of the LORD. (3:3)

The first time, Jonah "rose to flee" (1:3); this time he rises
to obey. He's finally behaving "according to the word of the
LORD"—that great pathway of highest adventure and fulfillment
for each and all of us.

What has happened to Jonah is a remarkable confirmation
of the truth of God's continuing guidance. In *Leading with a
Limp,* Dan Allender states it this way:

> When we hear the call to go and we run in the opposite direc-
> tion, God has a way of having us thrown off the boat, swal-
> lowed by a large fish, and spit onto the shore where we are
> to serve. God allows us to run and yet to know that he will
> arrive at our place of flight before we arrive, so he can direct
> our steps again.[7]

Jonah's strong will has been subdued and silenced. His
belated obedience is like the parable Jesus told about a father
with two sons: "He went to the first and said, 'Son, go and
work in the vineyard today.' And he answered, 'I will not,' but
afterward he changed his mind and went" (Matt. 21:28–29). It
has taken a lot to get Jonah to "change his mind," but at last
he has. Although delayed obedience is still disobedience at first,
it can be replaced by true obedience, through God's relentless
mercy and grace.

Jonah is also like John Mark, who once abandoned Paul and
his missionary work (Acts 15:37–38), yet Paul later asked for his
return—"for he is very useful to me for ministry" (2 Tim. 4:11).

Jonah will now be very useful in God's ministry to Nineveh, despite having earlier abandoned God.

But again, it's wise to remember from Scripture that second chances aren't guaranteed once we've disobeyed God in a certain matter the first time. Just ask Ananias and Sapphira (Acts 5). Or Lot's wife (Genesis 19). Or King Saul. When Saul disobeyed the Lord's guidelines for defeating and destroying the Amalekites, the prophet Samuel brought him a blistering response from God. Nothing matters more than obedience, Samuel told him; to disobey is "rebellion" and "presumption," and just as bad as idolatry. "Because you have rejected the word of the LORD, he has also rejected you from being king" (1 Sam. 15:22–23).

Saul had disobeyed, and so God fired him from his job as king. Jonah also disobeyed (perhaps even in a worse way than Saul did)—yet God did *not* fire Jonah from his job as prophet. It makes God's grace to Jonah look all the more mysterious and huge—and gracious.

NO GRUDGES

God's second commissioning of Jonah lets us glimpse three aspects of God's amazing grace.

First, God doesn't hold grudges. Sometimes we can learn a lot from what the Bible *doesn't* say. Even though the story doesn't tell us that Jonah ever confesses his wrongdoing or says he's sorry, God extends again to Jonah his call and mission. God doesn't remind Jonah of his past failings. His words carry no rebuke. Nor is there any sense here that God is thinking, *I know I'm going to regret this*—even though you and I must wonder: *Can God really trust this guy?*

For us, so many of our relationships—at work, in our families, with our friends and neighbors—eventually sour and spoil because of the grudges we hold. *You owe me, you've let me down, you've hurt me—so now I'm done with you.*

By holding grudges, we count others' sins against them. That's the terminology Paul uses when he says, "God . . . through Christ reconciled us to himself and gave us the ministry of reconciliation; that is, in Christ God was reconciling the world to himself, *not counting their trespasses against them*" (2 Cor. 5:18–19).

This is the gospel—the good news that God doesn't count our sins against us. So then, who *does* God count our sins against? Paul goes on to tell us: "For our sake he [God] made him [Christ] to be sin who knew no sin, so that in him we might become the righteousness of God" (5:21). This is what came to be called—from the days of the church fathers onward—the "great exchange" or the "glorious exchange." In his infinite mercy, God exchanged our corruption and sin for Christ's righteousness and perfection.

Here we see the stark difference between the way the world operates and how God operates. The world has no posture of grace in this regard. Everyone and everything in this world that you might give yourself to or entrust your heart to will eventually hold grudges against you, at some level, in some way. Your sins will be counted against you.

But the gospel gives us something remarkably different. Through the gospel God counts your sins against Christ, not against you. He offers us acceptance based not on what we do or don't do, but on what Christ has already done. It's an acceptance that can be neither gained by our achievements nor forfeited by our failures. Nothing in this world can promise you such total acceptance and favor—*nothing*. And that's what makes his grace so amazing.

NO DEALS

Notice also that God doesn't lighten the load for Jonah this second time around. He doesn't say, "Okay, I realize I gave you a pretty tall order that first time, and it was a bit out of reach for you, so let me make this a little easier for you. Let's throw in some adjustments so your success is guaranteed."

No, God doesn't budge. He doesn't negotiate. God is stable, consistent: "For I the LORD do not change" (Mal. 3:6). He won't bend to make our lives temporarily better when larger, longer-term issues are at stake.

If you want to live for things that bring only temporary comfort and happiness, there's plenty to choose from—plenty of ships sailing for Tarshish. Only God can take you beyond that—if you want to go beyond what you could ever become on your own.

God's grace isn't seen in the lessening of his demands toward us; he always has and always will demand perfect obedience. His grace is experienced when we come to realize that his perfect demands for each of us have already been met by Jesus. He lived the life we couldn't live and died the death we should have died.

This rescue doesn't come apart from God's law but rather in the perfect fulfillment of the law through the person of Jesus, who perfectly kept that law on behalf of sinners like you and me. Christianity is the only faith system where God both *makes* the demands and *meets* them.

Was it for crimes that I had done
He groaned upon the tree?
Amazing pity, grace unknown,
And love beyond degree![8]

GOD DOESN'T GIVE UP

God is more interested in the worker than he is in the work the worker does. He's more interested in *you* than in what you can accomplish. If accomplishing Project Nineveh was all God cared about, he could have discarded Jonah and found a more reliable prophet. He knew Jonah would run; so why did he ask Jonah to go in the first place? It was because *Jonah* was God's project. God comes after Jonah not because he needs Jonah, but because Jonah needs God.

All of us need to be continually rescued by God, whether from sin's power and presence, or also (once and for all) from its penalty. And one expression of God's amazing grace is that he pursues our rescue even though we cannot do one thing for him. God doesn't need you and me to increase his value and esteem. In and of himself he is already of infinite value and worth. The reason he seeks sinners, saves sinners, and sends sinners like Jonah (and like you and me) is that *God loves sinners*.

No other object of worship loves sinners like God does.

Jack Miller, a noted Presbyterian pastor and author in Philadelphia in the last century, often summed up the gospel this way: Cheer up; you're a lot worse off than you think you are, but in Jesus you're far more loved than you ever could have imagined.

Scene 3:

IN A GREAT CITY

When he [Jesus] saw the crowds, he had compassion for them,
because they were harassed and helpless, like sheep without a shepherd.

MATTHEW 9:36

⚓

Like a new person, Jonah "resolutely follows where the Lord leads," Calvin writes. The prophet "seems to have forgotten that he was an obscure man, alone, and unarmed; but he had laid hold on weapons capable of destroying all the power of the world, for he knew that he was sent from above. His conviction was that God was on his side, and he knew that God had called him."[1] Jonah was on the right road—and it was leading somewhere big.

TERRIBLY GREAT

This story never lets us lose sight of how vast Nineveh is. We're reminded again:

> Now Nineveh was an exceedingly great city, three days' journey in breadth. (3:3)

In Jonah's time, Nineveh was great in population, great in power, great in prestige, and great in importance.[2]

Greatness was Nineveh's destiny almost from the dawn of human history, as Jonah would know. We read about it way back in Genesis, in the era just after the great flood. Its founding is associated with Nimrod, Noah's great-grandson, who "was the first on earth to be a mighty man" (Gen. 10:8). Nimrod "went into Assyria and built Nineveh, Rehoboth-Ir, Calah, and Resen between Nineveh and Calah; *that is the great city*" (10:11–12). Both the "great city" wording in Genesis and the reference in Jonah to a city that was "three days' journey in breadth" may well refer to the larger urban district that included Nineveh and surrounding cities. Together they straddled both sides of the Tigris River around today's Mosul, Iraq's second largest city, about 250 miles upriver from Baghdad.

Calah, mentioned with Nineveh in Genesis 10, was especially important in Jonah's day. Nineveh and Calah were not many miles apart, and Assyria's kings built palaces in both places and governed their empire from both.

As Jonah approaches this urban expanse, his vision is filled with towers, temples, and city walls vastly larger than any he's ever seen. Doubtless he is awed. But most likely he is *not* thinking, "What a wonderfully gifted and resourceful people these Assyrians are, to produce such a grand and imposing metropolis." He would know that this immensity on display has come at a cruel price and is calculated not to win the world's admiration, but its fear.

It's safe to say that no people in all the span of biblical history had a worse reputation for brutality and arrogance than the Assyrians. This effect was intentional—part of their design that "featured deliberate terror and atrocity as instruments of foreign policy."[3] In the chronicles of their reigns, Assyria's kings boasted of their brutalities for everyone to read and hear about.

Leading the way was King Ashurnasirpal II, a century before Jonah's time. "I caused great slaughter," he wrote in describing a military campaign. "I destroyed, I demolished, I burned. I took their warriors prisoner and impaled them on stakes before their cities." He reported a battle where three thousand were killed and many others taken prisoner: "Many of the captives I burned in a fire. Many I took alive; from some I cut off their hands to the wrist, from others I cut off their noses, ears and fingers; I put out the eyes of many of the soldiers. I burnt their young men and women to death."[4]

After skinning alive some rebellious royal officials, Ashurnasirpal reports in detail—seemingly with cold pleasure—what he did with the human skins. Some he spread out on the pile of flayed corpses, some he placed on stakes driven amid the pile, while others were hung on stakes surrounding the pile. In other instances of flaying, he reports draping the human skins on walls, including Nineveh's walls. "Thus have I constantly established my victory and strength over the land," he concludes.[5]

Ashurnasirpal's policy continued to be followed by his successors, striking terror in the hearts of Assyria's neighbors. But every great power has moments of weakness, and Assyria was no exception. In the early to middle decades of the eighth century BC—the period when Jonah was a prophet—Assyria seemed weakened by a combination of factors, including drought and famine, intense military conflicts on the empire's northern border as well as uprisings within, a series of less capable kings, and even an earthquake and total solar eclipse, both viewed as tragic omens.[6] If ever there was a moment in the empire's history when a crack might open in her armor of arrogance and cruelty—perhaps this is it.

THE DOOM DELIVERED

Jonah enters vast Nineveh and starts doing what he came to do. He delivers the message God gave him.

> Jonah began to go into the city, going a day's journey. And he called out, "Yet forty days, and Nineveh shall be overthrown!" (3:4)

Only forty days. *Forty more days,* Jonah might be thinking, *and Assyria's threat to Israel will be ended forever.* Nineveh's legacy of brutal pride would be buried in the dust and ashes left by God's awful judgment.

Forty days. Jonah knows the biblical weight that number carries. For forty days the torrents of judgment fell in Noah's day to wipe out the wickedness of human life from the face of the earth (Gen. 7:12). Forty years in the wilderness was Israel's penalty for stiff-necked faithlessness (Num. 14:32–35) after God delivered her from Egypt—her crime so odious that God would say, "For forty years I loathed that generation" (Ps. 95:10). Forty stripes with the whip was the God-ordained penalty for a guilty man sentenced to a beating (Deut. 25:1–3).

Jonah would know: *"Forty days" shows that God means business, whether you people realize it or not.* Nineveh is doomed. Assyria will finally fall. Spurgeon pictures Jonah's proclamation this way:

He entered the city—perhaps he stood aghast for a moment at the multitude of its population, at its richness and splendor, but again he lilted up his sharp shrill voice, "Yet forty days and Nineveh shall be overthrown." On he went, and the crowd increased around him as he passed through each street, but they heard nothing but the solemn monotony, "Yet forty days and Nineveh shall be overthrown;" and yet again, "Yet forty days and Nineveh shall be overthrown."[7]

MESSAGE RECEIVED

In a book of Bible illustrations published three centuries ago,[8] a popular Dutch artist named Gerard Hoet portrays Jonah standing and preaching in the middle of mighty Nineveh. He is hooded, but his bearded face is visible; his expression is serious but not stern. His hands are raised, and one of them gestures heavenward.

All those around him are listening—intently, gravely. They kneel, they bow their heads, they swoon, they grimace. There's no sign of mocking, or hostility, or even indifference—any of which Jonah might easily expect as the Ninevites' response to his message. Instead, wonder of wonders, there's a total receptiveness.

> And the people of Nineveh believed God. They called for a fast and put on sackcloth, from the greatest of them to the least of them. (3:5)

It is *God*, not Jonah, whom they believe. In what the prophet is telling them, they recognize the voice of the Almighty—just as it should be with all God's messengers. And those in Nineveh who respond this way are not an isolated few, but a multitude.

Jesus would later say, "Jonah became a sign to the people of Nineveh" (Luke 11:30)—the prophet *himself* was the sign; he *became* that sign. H. L. Ellison pictures it this way:

> Jonah "proclaimed" his message. There may well have been something about Jonah, his bearing, his dress, or something else, as he strode toward the center of the city, looking neither to the right nor to the left, that drew many after him. When he finally stood and shouted, "Forty more days and Nineveh will be destroyed," the news spread like wildfire.[9]

Worthy of note is the content of Jonah's sermon. His eight-word sermon proves that, even though he complies with God's instruction to go to Nineveh this time around so as to avoid God's discipline, he hasn't had a change of heart. He is still the reluctant prophet who does not tell the Ninevites that there is a way out. All he preached was doom and gloom. There's no mention of even the possibility of forgiveness, because he didn't want the Ninevites to be saved. He wanted them to die. He hides from them the fact that while our sin reaches far, God's amazing grace reaches farther, and that God's willingness to forgive is infinitely bigger than our willingness to sin—something Jonah himself has just experienced. He's happy, in other words, to receive God's rescuing mercy, but he is not willing to extend God's rescuing mercy. One of the beauties of this story, however, is that in spite of the prophet's self-righteous reticence, the Ninevites repent anyway (and, as we'll see below, due to ignorance of what to do they even make their animals repent, but they are covering all their bases).

> The word reached the king of Nineveh, and he arose from his throne, removed his robe, covered himself with sackcloth, and sat in ashes. (3:6)

No one in Nineveh or outside it would ever picture an Assyrian ruler doing such a thing.[10]

The God who crafts storms and commands sea monsters is now doing something even more awesomely difficult: changing the hearts of sinful human beings. The king and the people's drastic and instant humbling of themselves is proof, Calvin says, "that God not only spoke by the mouth of Jonah but added power to his word." The king's reaction in particular is one that "must be ascribed to the hidden power of God."[11] Incredibly, the king goes still further.

> And he issued a proclamation and published through Nineveh, "By the decree of the king and his nobles: Let neither man nor beast, herd nor flock, taste anything. Let them not feed or drink water, but let man and beast be covered with sackcloth, and let them call out mightily to God. Let everyone turn from his evil way and from the violence that is in his hands. Who knows? God may turn and relent and turn from his fierce anger, so that we may not perish." (3:7–9)

Even the livestock in Nineveh—bawling and bleating from forced hunger and thirst—will share in this citywide plea to God, as the people "call out mightily" to him. We today might feel that forcing innocent animals to suffer along with the guilty people was unfair. But as Ellison reminds us, "The concept of a common Creator, today so often replaced by an impersonal idea of evolution, saw man and animal far more closely linked than does the modern concept of a purely biological link."[12]

Calvin explores the matter further. We must remember, he says, "that destruction had been denounced, not only on men, but also on the whole city." Without God's intervention, the cattle and sheep and goats will all die in forty days, just as the men and women and children will. Moreover, in depriving the animals, the king would actually have in mind its effect on the people: seeing and hearing an afflicted ox or lamb or goat, its human caretakers would be reminded "of what grievous and severe punishment they were worthy, inasmuch as innocent animals suffered punishment together with them." The king's hope was that "men were roused by such means seriously to acknowledge the wrath of God, and to entertain greater fear, that they might be more truly humbled before him, and be displeased with themselves, and be thus more disposed and better prepared and molded to seek pardon."[13]

Whether by human intention or not, and whether we think it's fair or not, animals and all the rest of creation have been stuck with the curse of suffering brought by mankind's sinfulness, as Paul reminds us in Romans 8:20–22. It's not just Nineveh's animals that are moaning; "*the whole creation* has been groaning together" (8:22).

WHO KNOWS?

The king doesn't defend Nineveh by saying her people are undeserving of God's promised wrath; no, he acknowledges that "evil" and "violence" are on every man's hands. Therefore he insists that the people do much more than pray. They must all rid themselves of their sinful deeds. Every Ninevite individually is to "bear fruit in keeping with repentance," to borrow John the Baptist's words (Matt. 3:8); or to quote the gospel-preaching Paul, they must "repent and turn to God, performing deeds in keeping with their repentance" (Acts 26:20).

This is the hour of truth for Nineveh. The king understands a universal fact: *when God has fierce anger toward any of his created beings, they can rightly expect to perish.* The king totally gets it. "He and the city are linked together and share in the same fate," Ellison observes. "A city and its king have to act, and according to their action so will be their fate."[14]

What will that fate be? "Who knows?" the king says. Will God have mercy? Who *does* know that, in any particular situation in this world? We sense great emphasis and significance in this question asked by the king. Could this be a clue to what the book of Jonah is all about?

Who knows? It was the same question that David asked, when he fasted and wept and worshiped and prayed because his newborn son—a child conceived in adultery—was dying. "Who knows whether the LORD will be gracious to me, that the child may live?" (2 Sam. 12:22). In David's case, the child died. Will Nineveh's king and people and animals also die? They do not know. So an entire city responds—king and commoner, from the greatest to the least. Everyone fasts, cries out to God, renounces sin, and waits.

In all the great cities in all of human history, has such a thing ever happened?

ABUNDANT PARDON

By his sure and sovereign word, God had promised Nineveh's destruction. But the surprises in this story just won't end.

> When God saw what they did, how they turned from their evil way, God relented of the disaster that he had said he would do to them, and he did not do it. (3:10)

Nineveh had known that God their creator was mindful enough of them to send them his prophet and his warning. It gave them hope—and that hope is fulfilled. Now, from personal experience, they know the beginnings of a fuller truth:

> Seek the LORD while he may be found;
> call upon him while he is near;
> let the wicked forsake his way,
> and the unrighteous man his thoughts;
> let him return to the LORD,
> that he may have compassion on him,
> and to our God,
> for he will abundantly pardon. (Isa. 55:6–7)

Nineveh knows: God's compassion, his grace, his pardon—they're utterly shocking in their abundance. Nineveh is spared!

GOD USES THE DEFEATED TO DO GREAT THINGS

We've seen how that word *great* (*gadol*) plays such a key role in the telling of this story. One of the stylistic features of the book of Jonah is its "giantesque motif";[15] nothing that happens is insignificant; everything's bigger than expected. That theme continues here in the Nineveh scene. Just as the task assigned to Jonah was large, and the storm was large, and the fear of the sailors was large, so also the effect of Jonah's sermon is large; the turnaround in Nineveh is huge—perhaps the greatest revival that history has ever seen. God has thoroughly humbled a violently arrogant city; he has resurrected a spiritually dead city; and it happens to be the most powerful metropolis in the world.

And yet, as his instrument to bring this about, he has used a failure, a runaway, a washed-up prophet.

If you're a football coach, and your team is facing the biggest play of their biggest game, do you give the ball to the guy who just fumbled it and killed your last scoring drive? If you own a business, and you're trying to win over your biggest account ever, do you give responsibility for it to the guy on the sales staff whose incompetence just drove away another big customer? That's essentially what God is doing with Jonah.

Why? Because God has a remarkable work to do not only in Nineveh but also in Jonah. And he operates according to a completely different value system from the way we normally coach teams and manage businesses and run our lives in this world.

Jonah has just emerged from the lowest experience of his life, being stuck for days in the belly of a fish. He must be thoroughly and absolutely convinced by now that trying to run from God is futile. He's a defeated man. His words to God in his psalm, expressing such amazed gratitude over his deliverance, seem to show that he's definitely learned this lesson: *God is God, and I am not. God is big, and I am small.*

And that's the secret. When we realize that he's God and we're not—that he's massive and we're minute—that's all it takes for us to become a part of great and powerful God-things. *God chooses defeated people to do dominant things.* Unimaginable, undreamed-of accomplishments and experiences await those who'll recognize and admit just how small they are. Both the Bible and church history show that God does everything through those who understand they are nothing, and God does nothing through those who think they are everything. As G. K. Chesterton put it, "How much larger your life would be if your self could become smaller in it."[16]

This makes Christianity a unique and liberating breath of fresh air. Why? Because this world values the dominant, not the defeated. Everything in this world caters to the beautiful people. Our world says that for you to be valuable, you must be healthy, attractive, prosperous, and influential. To be useful, you must become powerful. The world and all its religions say, "You must *become* great before you can *do* great." But this story shows us that in God's eyes, and in Christianity, weakness precedes usefulness.

"Jonah stands as the great example of human weakness in the chosen instruments of God's hand"[17]—so wrote Scottish-born Baptist preacher Alexander Maclaren, who himself was one of those chosen instruments, second only to his friend Charles Spurgeon in his fame as a preacher in nineteenth-century Britain.

GOOD NEWS FOR LOSERS

The way God mightily used a weakened Jonah is a foreshadowing of how Christ accomplished his work of redemption: "For he was crucified *in weakness,* but lives by the power of God" (2 Cor. 13:4). In the cross, Jesus proves that there's great power in defeat. Christ, "though he was in the form of God," became small—"made himself nothing, taking the form of a servant, being born in the likeness of men" (Phil. 2:6–7). He thereby accomplished a cosmic rescue, the greatest feat in human history: his magnificent defeat on the cross guaranteed the elimination of sin and death. His loss guaranteed that one day every wrong will be righted and every tear wiped away.

People were offended back when media mogul Ted Turner called Christianity "a religion for losers" (he later expressed regret for that and similar remarks).[18] But the fact is, in one sense Ted Turner was exactly right. Christianity *is* for losers.

For a long time, we Christians have spent time and energy and money trying our best to convince the world we're cool, and that we're winners. And in our world, *cool* means being just as prominent and prosperous, just as smart and stylish, just as successful and savvy as anybody else. Just look at how Christians swell with pride when a successful athlete or actor or politician professes his faith. It's as if we shout to everyone, "*See!* This guy has everything, and *he's* a believer—so Christianity has to be cool." We want to parade these celebrities and their faith before the world.

In *Too Good to Be True,* Michael Horton asks, "Have you ever seen a janitor interviewed for his testimony?"[19] The reason we haven't is that God-fearing janitors don't represent strength or intelligence or coolness in our culture. They're viewed as less valuable than the famous entertainer or the sports star or the rising politician. And we, as the church, have adopted the same categorization.

The gospel, however, is not just for the all-star and the illustrious and the legendary. It's for the loser. It's for the defeated, not the dominant. It's for those who realize they're unable to carry the weight of the world on their shoulders—those who've figured out that they're not gods. It's for people who understand the bankruptcy of life without God. It's for people who recognize that while they're definitely deficient, God is more than sufficient.

Jesus came to show us that the gospel explains success in terms of giving, not taking; self-sacrifice, not self-protection; going to the back, not getting to the front. The gospel shows that we win by losing, we triumph through defeat, we achieve power through service, and we become rich by giving ourselves away.

In fact, in gospel-centered living we follow Jesus in laying down our lives for those who hate us and hurt us. We spend our lives serving instead of being served, and seeking last place, not first. Gospel-centered people are those who love giving up their place for others, not guarding their place from others—because their value and worth is found in Christ, not their position.

Do you remember, in Gethsemane, when Jesus told Peter to put away his sword (Matt. 26:52)? He did this to show us that in God's economy, winning this battle involves dying rather than killing.

When we understand that our significance and identity are in Christ, we don't have to win—we're free to lose. The gospel frees us from the pressure to generate our own significance and meaning. In Christ, our identity and significance are secure, which frees us up to give everything we have, because in Christ we have everything we need.

The gospel is for the strong and mighty (like the Ninevites) *only* when they're humbled and repentant. That's why Paul says that "God chose what is foolish in the world to shame the wise; God chose what is weak in the world to shame the strong" (1 Cor. 1:27).

The gospel is good news for losers. Jesus lived the life we losers couldn't live and died the death we losers should have died.

> In my place condemned he stood,
> sealed my pardon with his blood.
> Hallelujah! What a Savior![20]

In the end, in the bigger story, God emerges as the sole superstar, the sole hero. Through Christ and the gospel, he alone is the great victor.

EVERY SOLUTION

The place where God sent his weak servant Jonah was the very stronghold of darkness. Nineveh represented the sin center of the world. Everything godless happened there; by all accounts its people were perverse, sadistic, and evil. The very fact that Jonah was even sent to such a place reveals that God's capacity to forgive is greater than our capacity to sin. And because of God, all the Ninevites turned from their wicked ways and placed their trust in his mercy. Everyone *repented*, from the least to the greatest—from the kids to the king.

I want to suggest that repentance like that is the solution for every social and relational disease in our world today. Wherever there's a social or relational problem, it's because repentance is missing. I know that's a big statement. So I want to prove it by exploring what repentance is and what repentance does.

WHAT REPENTANCE IS

Bible teachers often distinguish between two kinds of repentance. The first kind is what they call *attrition*. It isn't heartfelt sorrow for wrongdoing but a selfishly motivated response to potential punishment. This could well be Jonah's response. His willingness to go to Nineveh now in order to avoid further discipline can be seen as an act of attrition—external, self-preserving, and even self-centered.

The second kind of repentance Bible teachers talk about is *contrition*. Contrition is true repentance. It entails heartfelt sorrow for offending God and others. It involves not just turning *away from* disobedience, but also turning *toward* obedience. It's an external change motivated by an internal change. It's self-sacrificial. It's God-centered.

False repentance, or no repentance, leads to bitterness, anger, and unwillingness to acknowledge wrongdoing. Until we can recognize our own wrongdoing, we'll continue to be mastered by this self-centered bondage. Our relationships will continue to be strained and frayed. Freedom comes only with true repentance.

WHAT REPENTANCE DOES

My take on this part of the story is that the Ninevites didn't simply turn away from disobedience but turned toward obedience. They acknowledged their wrongdoing and sought restitution with God and one another. Nobody was crying out, "This is all your fault." Rather, they were crying out, "This is all my fault." They were no longer proud; they were humble. That's what true repentance requires.

When true repentance is offered, God promises to forgive and restore. This proves that Nineveh's repentance was true, because God forgave and restored. True repentance is the means by which God brings about real restoration, a restoration that brings the deepest experience of peace.

The Old Testament word for peace is *shalom,* but this Hebrew term carries a richer meaning than the English word. *Shalom* means much more than peace of mind, a ceasefire between enemies, or inner calmness. It means universal flourishing and wholeness. It means things are complete and settled. *Shalom* is the way things ought to be—the way God intended things to be. This is why one writer defines sin as "the vandalism of shalom."[21]

Sin twists and corrupts things; it brings brokenness to our lives and this world. *Shalom* straightens things out and cleanses things. *Shalom* brings healing and restoration. It reweaves the fraying fabric of our lives and this world. This, I believe, is what's happening in Nineveh. Their wickedness had caused the fabric of their lives and city to fray, to come unraveled. They hear Jonah's message, they repent, and *shalom* begins to reweave the fabric of their lives and their city. Relational ills and social ills can now begin to dissipate. *Shalom* comes only through repentance. Repentance is the hose that *shalom* flows through. When the hose is kinked, *shalom* doesn't flow.

The prophet Isaiah tells us that God's plan is to bring peace on earth through his appointed king. This coming king will be "Prince of Peace," and "of the increase of his government and of peace there will be no end" (Isa. 9:6–7). Likewise the king of Nineveh's leadership and his example of repentance have caused God's grace and peace to flow throughout the city. God's peace has become a part of everything Nineveh is about. The city is turned upside down, as real revival takes place. In this way the king of Nineveh points us to Christ the king.

As we read the Gospels, we see that Christ is the administrator of this peace. He's the one who sets things straight. He's the one who comes to clean things up. He's the one who brings restoration to our lives and to this world. He took on human flesh and frailties in order to repair *shalom*. He came to reweave the fraying fabric of our lives and this world.

NINEVEH'S FATHER

Like the father's treatment of the prodigal in the story Jesus told, so has God been a father to Nineveh—to the city that previously led the world in prideful, sinful arrogance and violence.

In one of his songs, David showed that he could look beyond the borders of Israel when he wrote, "How precious is your steadfast love, O God! *The children of mankind* take refuge in the shadow of your wings" (Ps. 36:7). The people of Nineveh were getting a taste of the preciousness of that love and the safety of that refuge.

Why did God show such graciousness to Nineveh—to such a wicked city? Maybe that's just the point. Paul once called himself the foremost of sinners. "But I received mercy for this reason, that in me, as the foremost, Jesus Christ might display his perfect patience as an example to those who were to believe in him for eternal life" (1 Tim. 1:15–16). The God who would save the worst of sinners had now spared the worst of cities. We can detect the same intention in God's heart in both cases.

And what would happen next for Nineveh? As for Paul, he

could testify, "By the grace of God I am what I am, and his grace toward me was not in vain. On the contrary, I worked harder than any of them, though it was not I, but the grace of God that is with me" (1 Cor. 15:10). Will God's mercy toward Nineveh be as effective and as productive as it was for Paul? Or will it be in vain?

Surprisingly, the story of Jonah has different questions to address, and a different direction to follow, as we quickly learn. God isn't finished with Jonah—or with us.

Scene 4:

IN A GREAT RAGE

*But I say to you, Love your enemies and pray for those
who persecute you.*
JESUS, IN MATTHEW 5:44

⚓

Nineveh has repented before God, and he has spared
this great city from his wrath. For the first time, we
see Jonah's reaction:

But it displeased Jonah exceedingly, and he was angry. (4:1)

Whoa, what's this? Jonah is vexed in a big way, and it's boiling
up into rage. Whatever for?

And he prayed to the LORD and said, "O LORD, is not this
what I said when I was yet in my country? That is why
I made haste to flee to Tarshish; for I knew that you are a
gracious God and merciful, slow to anger and abounding in
steadfast love, and relenting from disaster." (4:2)

This has to be the most bewildering thing in the entire story.

HATING GOD
At last we're hearing straight from Jonah's own mouth the
reason he fled from God in the first place. It wasn't that he

feared failure in the task God gave him; it was because he feared *success*.

Even back then—even before his personal experience of God's merciful rescue through the great fish—he knew God well enough to realize the Lord's compassion toward Nineveh would trigger her repentance and allow her to escape his wrath. He knew this was why God was sending a prophet to Nineveh with a message of doom. And Jonah hated the thought of it.

Suddenly the story shifts into a new dimension. New questions assault our minds, especially this one: How can Jonah be so upset over God's mercy? It's like he's stomping his feet and railing away at God: "I *knew* it! I just *knew* it!" It looks so pathetic. It seems like such silly peevishness—or maybe even a touch of insanity. But he's not insane. There has to be something deeper going on here.

In 4:1, the opening phrase in this scene about Jonah's displeasure could be translated more literally, "But it was *evil* to Jonah, with great [*gadol*] *evil.*" Bible scholars tell us that the Hebrew form employed here has a wide range of meaning, including not only "evil" and "displeasure" but also "calamity," "trouble," "harm," and more.[1] It's translated mostly as "evil" in Jonah; the exceptions include here in 4:1 ("it *displeased* Jonah") and in 3:10 and 4:2, where it's the "disaster" that God relented from bringing upon Nineveh. The use of this word helps us see the real intensity and depth of Jonah's inner state here. He's not just bothered; this is something deeply offensive and troubling to him.

In the qualities Jonah ascribes here to God—grace, mercy, slowness to anger, steadfast love—he's right on. These are the very things God has revealed about himself, long ago on

Mount Sinai, in a time of great distress and confusion for God's people. It was right after they'd sinned by making a golden calf and worshiping it. God threatened to no longer go with them in their journey to the Promised Land. On their behalf, Moses pleaded with God to change his mind. God listened and agreed. This emboldened Moses to ask for something more, something personal: "Please show me your glory" (Ex. 33:18).

God's answer was deep and involved. Moses wouldn't be allowed to see God's face, because that was too dangerous. It would kill Moses. But God promised to let him glimpse "all my goodness," and to hear him proclaim his name. God also added this statement about his sovereign purposes and control—and it's a line for the ages: "I will be gracious to whom I will be gracious, and will show mercy on whom I will show mercy" (Ex. 33:19).

Then God put Moses in a crevice in a rock, and "passed before him" while Moses heard these words:

> The LORD, the LORD, a God merciful and gracious, slow
> to anger, and abounding in steadfast love and faithfulness.
> (Ex. 34:6)

Those words, freighted with meaning, were pressed deep into Israel's consciousness of God. David, for example, repeated them often (as in Pss. 86:5, 15; 103:8; and 145:8).

Jonah, too, remembers those words—and *doesn't like what they say!* He just doesn't agree with how God does things. "What is clear," H. L. Ellison writes, "is that Jonah was finding fault with God as he really is, not as he imagined him to be."[2] Douglas Stuart expresses it more bluntly: "It was not simply

. . . that Jonah could not bring himself to appreciate Nineveh. Rather, to a shocking extent, he could not stand God!"[3]

Well at least he's being honest, we might say. Yes, surely it's better for Jonah to admit how he feels—and to purposely pray about it—than to try to hide or disguise his feelings from God. So will *we* be just as honest about ourselves? Instead of taking God as he is, Jonah would rather remake God in his own image. Don't we all try that at times?

AN EXCUSE FOR NO CONFESSION

As Jonah pours out his aversion to what God has done with Nineveh, he adds this self-condemning phrase: "That is why I made haste to flee to Tarshish." When he first heard God's call, if he'd expected Nineveh to actually be destroyed, he probably would have hurried there to give them God's message and seal the deal. But he knew God's character too well to believe that. He strongly suspected that announcing doom to Nineveh would actually bring about their repentance and deliverance—and Jonah wanted no part of that.

When he finally went to Nineveh, it was only because God supernaturally forced him into it. And once he was there, it's easy to imagine Jonah pronouncing God's coming wrath with flowing ease and bold authority, while keeping a tight-lipped silence about any chance that Nineveh might experience God's mercy—the thought of which was so repulsive to Jonah.

But whatever Jonah's motives or methods or mind games, God sovereignly orchestrated the result he'd always intended from his prophet's proclamation—Nineveh's God-fearing, brokenhearted contrition. It was precisely the outcome Jonah feared but proved powerless to prevent. Perhaps the likelihood of it gnawed at his guts with every word he spoke in Nineveh's streets. Or maybe he deluded himself to think that after all the trouble he'd experienced, God owed him the favor of wiping out Nineveh exactly as Jonah wished. Yet it wasn't to be.

Now we can better understand why we haven't heard any confession of wrongdoing from Jonah about his going AWOL from God. Jonah has *always* felt totally justified in having run away from this assignment—more justified now than ever, it seems. *See! I've been right all along!* His worst fears have come true. In his mind, events have played out according to the worst-case scenario he'd already imagined. The very circumstances he did his darnedest to head off have happened anyway. Jonah may as well be shouting in God's face: "If I could do all this over again, I'd *still* run away from you—faster and farther!"

Jonah's stubborn guilt is summed up by these words in one commentary: "When men insist that they have done right, and call up sins which should have been forgotten, and for which they have been chastised, they display ignorance, pride, and self-conceit."[4] That's Jonah, all right.

MIGHT AS WELL DIE

"This is monstrous," Calvin says of Jonah's response that's revealed here.[5] But the prophet keeps protesting.

> Therefore now, O LORD, please take my life from me, for it is better for me to die than to live. (4:3)

He's serious. Jonah means this with all his heart. He's *had it* with God. God's answer to Jonah's protest has an air of mystery.

And the LORD said, "Do you do well to be angry?" (4:4)

It had seemed, back inside the great fish, that Jonah had prayed so well and praised God so well. And in Nineveh he'd prophesied well for God. But suddenly, here's all this hot anger as he talks with God. Is it really necessary? *Jonah, why are you doing this to yourself?*

Ellison suggests this translation for God's question here: "Are you right to be angry?" *Are you sure you've gauged this situation accurately?* "God was not rebuking Jonah," Ellison says; "God was not even asking him what right he, a man, had to criticize God. Rather he was suggesting to him that he might not be correct in his estimate of the position."[6]

Here's yet another mark of God's compassion in how he treats his prophet.

BACK TO THE BELLY: A REASSESSMENT

Jonah's startling words in this scene force us back to Jonah's psalm, to reexamine and question what we heard Jonah praying in the fish's belly.

To be fair, we have to assume Jonah sincerely meant what he said in that prayer. Here was faith, demonstrated and proven. Yet true faith—for Jonah and for all of us—always carries the dynamics of *more to learn* and *more to be surprised by*. That's because true faith brings us to a better and closer view of God's character, and his character is so different from ours that an ever-closer view of it will never cease to astonish us. No one, not even an obedient and successful prophet, can ever have God fully scoped out. Faith, in fact, trusts God even when it cannot trace him. There's always more to learn about him. If we aren't growing in our faith by learning more about God, there's only stagnation and decline.

As one commentary sums it up, Jonah's psalm "is a moving testimony to the heart of Israel's faith and to the heart of the prophet, but he still had much to learn. His vision of God's mercy was still narrow."[7]

Jonah's genuine respect for God's Word and God's people isn't something that's wrong on its own. What makes it deficient—and deplorable—is that it doesn't keep the living God at the center; instead it tries to keep God in a box in the corner.

"There is but one good," C. S. Lewis writes in *The Great Divorce;* "that is God. Everything else is good when it looks to Him and bad when it turns from Him."[8] When God's actions show that he's totally outside the box Jonah constructed for him, Jonah can't handle that. It's so crushing for him, so hurtful, that he's infuriated. His reaction proves that in his religiousness and spirituality, he's lost sight of God. He can *say* the ancient formula, and he knows it intellectually—*God is gracious and merciful, slow to anger and abounding in steadfast love.* But in his heart, Jonah doesn't *really* see it enough to trust and embrace and celebrate it.

A FURTHER RESCUE

Looking back, it becomes obvious that even in his prayer inside the fish, Jonah still doesn't get it. Yes, he triumphantly declares that "salvation belongs to the Lord!" (2:9). And yes, Jonah has been saved. Yet *he still needs to be saved.*

The word *salvation* in the Bible literally means "rescue."

But in regard to being rescued from sin, the Bible uses this term in different ways. It can mean (1) your one-time deliverance from sin's eternal penalty, (2) your ongoing liberation from sin's power in your remaining time in this life, and (3) your final freedom in eternity from sin's presence altogether.

If you don't have a relationship with God through faith in Jesus Christ, you still need all three forms of rescue. If you do have that relationship, then even though you've already experienced the first form of God's rescue, you're still in need of the other two.

Paul calls the gospel "the power of God unto salvation," and contrary to what some have concluded, he didn't simply mean the "power of God unto conversion." The gospel remains the power of God unto salvation until we are glorified. We need God's rescue every day and in every way because we are, in the words of John Calvin, "partly unbelievers until we die." This is Jonah. He's still clearly in need of some rescue—and God shows how he's still at work to make it happen.

Believing fully the truth that *salvation belongs to the Lord* means that you place ultimate trust in Christ's efforts, not your own. You understand that seeking deliverance and freedom in anything else but God leads only to breakdown and slavery, because we were *made* for God. As Tim Keller reminds us, "When a fish leaves the water, which he was built for, he is not free, but dead."[9] Living for anything else besides God leads to death, not freedom.

Augustine's words at the beginning of his *Confessions* are forever true: "You made us for yourself, and our hearts are restless until they rest in you."[10] *That's why so many people who have achieved so much are unsatisfied, still looking for more, for something else. They're looking to things that can never deliver fulfillment—things that were never meant to be "gods," to replace the true God.*

IDOLATRY

We also find ourselves taking a second look at Jonah's statement inside the fish that "those who pay regard to vain idols forsake their hope of steadfast love" (2:8).

What Jonah apparently doesn't realize is that he, too, is an idol worshiper—and therefore, by his own assertion, forfeiting any claim to God's grace. The idols Jonah worships may look different on the surface from those worshiped by the sailors back on the ship or by the people he saw in the streets of Nineveh, but they're essentially no different. They're all competitors with the only true God.

We especially sense the idolatry of Jonah's Hebrew nationalism and religious elitism as we hear his adamant disagreement with God over Nineveh's pardon. Now it makes more sense why the first words spoken from Jonah's mouth in this book, and his first words of confession when he's pressured to fully identify himself, are these: "I am a Hebrew" (1:9).

OUR WORSHIP AND OUR FEARS

Ultimately, Jonah's condition is something everyone experiences. All of us are worshipers—of *something*. It's that simple. We're created, designed, and wired for worship. Being human *is* to be a worshiper. It's one of the biggest distinctives that mark us as human beings in this universe filled with living creatures.

The English word *worship* derives from the idea of *"worth-*

ship," meaning that we all serve those things to which we attribute ultimate worth. Worship is a posture of the heart. It is an attitude of loyalty and trust toward something—someone—in your life that you believe makes life worth living. Ultimately, worship defines you, makes your life meaningful, and gives you security. Thus, we all worship something or someone. This is true whether you consider yourself to be religious or not, spiritual or not, Christian or not. They're who you're depending on to give your life meaning. Typically, whatever we worship is our "nonnegotiable." It is that one thing, should we lose it or part with it, which would bring both devastation and hopelessness.

What you choose to attribute ultimate worth to—what you choose to worship—depends on what you *fear* the most. If you fear loneliness, you worship relationships. You depend on them to save you from a meaningless life. If you fear not being accepted or esteemed, you worship your social network, the way you look, the car you drive, or the amount of money you make. You depend on these things to validate your existence. If you fear insignificance, you end up worshiping your career or your accomplishments.

Behind everything you worship is some fear that, without this person or thing, you'd be lost. Life wouldn't be worth living. Your fears cause you to attribute ultimate worth either to things such as success, reputation, family, relationships, or to God. Either you believe your life would be meaningless without your friends, or your career achievement, or your children, or your possessions, or your social status, or whatever, or you believe your life wouldn't be worth living without God, because you know he alone can provide everything you need (and, in fact, long for)—justification, love, mercy, grace, cleansing, a new beginning, eternal approval and acceptance, righteousness, and rescue. We're all worshipers—but God is the only reliable object of worship because nothing and no one extends these things like God does in the person and work of Jesus Christ.

According to the Bible, anything we worship—other than God himself—is an idol. Idolatry is centering our attention and affection on something, or someone, smaller than God. In fact, most idols are good things in our lives that we turn into ultimate things, things that take God's place as we unconsciously depend on them to give our lives meaning and security. This is what John Calvin meant when he said that the human heart is an idol-making factory—taking good things and making them into idols that end up defining us.

Idolatry is trying to build our identity around something besides God. And this is not just a problem for non-Christians; it's a problem for Christians too. Christians also are guilty of trusting in things smaller than God to give their lives meaning and significance. We look to our achievements, our reputation, our relationships, our strengths, our place in society, our stuff, our smarts, our good looks, and on and on it goes. So, let's not make the mistake (like Jonah does here) of thinking that idolatry is only a non-Christian problem.

Jonah doesn't get all this. He has depended on his unique national and religious pedigree to give his life meaning. *His identity is not anchored in God, but in being an Israelite and a prophet.* That's why he runs when God asks him to go to his enemies and allow them, through God's message and merciful intervention, to experience the grace of God that Jonah himself has experienced. It's as if Jonah says, "What would set *me* apart, if the Ninevites had what I had? There would be nothing left to make me unique." This fear of losing his unique identity leads him to idolize his pedigree.

How about you? What is it that, if you were to lose it, would cause you to feel that life isn't worth living? In other words, what are your idols? What do you trust in other than Jesus to gain acceptance and approval—to give your life meaning and to make life worth living? All of us try to stand on any of an endless catalog of God-replacements that will only end up sinking beneath us, incapable of providing the "solid rock" of meaning and validation that we crave.

Experiencing God's deep rescue begins with identifying what idols you worship.

MOTIVES

We can see now that although Jonah at last went to Nineveh and preached the message God gave him, his motives and attitude and intentions appear to be about as far from God's as they could possibly be. So there's such a thing as running from God in our obedience as well as in our disobedience. Even when Jonah obeys God's call, it becomes clear that his heart's not in it.

It's possible to do the right thing with the wrong heart—and when we do that, it proves we don't know the heart of God.

Jonah is like the Pharisees of Jesus' day, with all their meticulous, self-righteous rule keeping that totally missed God's intentions and the spirit of his laws. One thing the Bible makes clear is that self-righteousness is the premier enemy of the gospel, and no one in the Bible better embodies that sin than the Pharisees. If Jonah had lived on earth in the same timeframe as Jesus, we could easily picture him in the thick of things with the Pharisees, walking their walk and talking their talk. He would thus share in the same indictment they received from Jesus' lips: "Woe to you . . . hypocrites! For you are like whitewashed tombs" (Matt. 23:27).

True obedience in the Bible never means mere external compliance to God's rules. Obedience that honors God flows from a heart that loves him and wants nothing more than to please him by doing everything he asks.

And yet, although Jonah's obedience was so flawed, *God still used him* to accomplish his purpose in Nineveh. That should continue to encourage us.

I know that if I waited to preach week after week until I knew my motives were absolutely 100 percent pure, I'd never do it. In fact, let me help to liberate you right now. If you're waiting to make a decision or to step forward in obedience to God's guidance because you want to make sure your motives are perfectly pure—you'll be waiting until you die. Your motives will always have a little self-centeredness mixed in. That's just part of sin's effect on all of us. There'll always be pride coloring our actions, however big or small those actions are.

IN ANGER'S TRAP

Jonah's outrage is like that of the older brother in the parable of the prodigal son. Hearing that his father was throwing a party for the reckless younger son, the older one "was angry and refused to go in." But the father, showing compassion equally to both, "came out and entreated him" (Luke 15:28).

So in Jonah's story—will God "come out" to him now and entreat his sulking servant? That's the only way out of this for

Jonah. He thinks he's right to be angry, but "the anger of man does not produce the righteousness of God" (James 1:20). Jonah is biting the hand that feeds him. God is Jonah's only hope, his only source of peace and joy. Only God can free Jonah from slavery to self-reliance, which is causing him such misery.

God is staying involved with Jonah because he wants Jonah to experience deliverance from his desperation. He wants to calm his fury; he wants to help him and teach him.

He'll now go about it in a strange and unforgettable way.

Scene 5:

OUTSIDE AND ALONE

The LORD is gracious and merciful,
slow to anger and abounding in steadfast love.
The LORD is good to all, and his mercy is over all that he has made.

PSALM 145:8—9

⚓

God's question to his angry prophet—essentially, "Are you sure your reaction is the right one?"—may have led Jonah to hope that judgment will pour down on Nineveh after all.

> Jonah went out of the city and sat to the east of the city and made a booth for himself there. He sat under it in the shade, till he should see what would become of the city. (4:5)

He doesn't stay in the city as God's servant to help those who have repented. "He does not lead the Ninevites in prayer, encourage them to continue and deepen their commitment to God. . . . Instead of working to shape events, Jonah is content to find a secluded place, pout, and watch events unfold."[1]

He's outside this city he despises, and he's alone—by choice. Understandably, given those hot desert lands under a beating sun, Jonah contrives a shelter. He wants to be comfortable while he waits and watches.

A PLANT FROM GOD

But God doesn't leave Jonah to himself. Instead, he helps Jonah find comfort.

> Now the LORD God appointed a plant and made it come up over Jonah, that it might be a shade over his head, to save him from his discomfort. So Jonah was exceedingly glad because of the plant. (4:6)

Jonah was "exceedingly displeased" earlier; now he's "exceedingly glad" because the shelter of his little hut is amplified by this shady plant springing up out of nowhere. It was God-appointed—one more expression of the Lord's endless grace toward his prophet.

Interestingly, the word translated "discomfort" here is again that expressive Hebrew term used for "evil" and "trouble" and "harm"—the same term used twice in verse 1 of Jonah 4, where we first saw Jonah's reaction to Nineveh's deliverance: literally, "But it was evil to Jonah, with great evil." Our abundantly gracious God wants to pull Jonah out from under this oppressive weight he feels. He sends the shade-giving plant—and it works. Suddenly Jonah is over-the-top delighted.

As represented in art over the ages, the image of Jonah under the shade plant (often seen as a gourd plant, or some other plant with large leaves) is characterized by carefree comfort. Carved into a third-century stone coffin found in Italy is a figure of Jonah in naked repose under the hanging gourds, with his legs crossed and one bent arm resting lazily atop his head. He looks down to where the fingers of his other hand touch the ground, as if he's doodling in the desert sand.[2] Meanwhile, in a seventeenth-century stained glass window in Christ Church Cathedral in Oxford, England, Jonah is royally attired in a deep-blue robe. Under a luxurious, tree-like gourd plant, he rests his bearded chin on his knuckles, and casts a calm gaze in the direction of distant Nineveh.[3]

A WORM AND A WIND FROM GOD

But Jonah's comfort won't last. For Jonah's higher good, God has more "appointing" to do.

> But when dawn came up the next day, God appointed a worm that attacked the plant, so that it withered. (4:7)

The Lord gave, and the Lord has taken away. A mere worm sabotages Jonah's lush shade. Then God sends something more.

> When the sun rose, God appointed a scorching east wind, and the sun beat down on the head of Jonah so that he was faint. And he asked that he might die and said, "It is better for me to die than to live." (4:8)

The shady plant had been proof of God's love, but so were the killing worm and the scorching wind, because "the Lord disciplines the one he loves, and chastises every son whom he receives" (Heb. 12:6). But Jonah doesn't see it that way.

A compelling and sympathetic view of Jonah at this stage of the story has been provided for us by the distinguished twentieth-century artist Eugen Spiro, known for his portraits of Albert Einstein and many notable European musicians and other personalities. Spiro was a Jew who fled Nazi Germany in the 1930s for Paris, where he helped form the Union of Free Artists. He was forced to flee again after the fall of France to the Nazis in 1940; the following year, at the age of sixty-seven, he arrived in the United States. Spiro painted a series of portraits of the biblical prophets. In the background of his painting of Jonah, we see the wilted plant, plus Nineveh's wall and buildings in the background. In the foreground, most of the painting is taken up by the figure of Jonah, leaning back. We see his bare chest and shoulders and his face of suffering. His eyes are closed, his brow tightened in pain, his mouth open as if in a groan. In a gesture of supplication, one hand is raised at his shoulder; the other is palm-up below his chest. He looks ready to end it all.[4]

In asking to die, Jonah may feel he's following in the footsteps of the great prophet Elijah in the previous century. During the reign of the evil King Ahab and his wicked wife Jezebel, Elijah was on the run after his successful confrontation with their false prophets. He fled into the wilderness "and came and sat down under a broom tree. And he asked that he might die, saying, 'It is enough; now, O LORD, take away my life'" (1 Kings 19:4). But in Jonah's case, nobody's chasing him—except, of course, God.

> But God said to Jonah, "Do you do well to be angry for the plant?" (4:9)

It's not despair that's driving Jonah's heart, but anger again. In his reaction to the plant, we sense his idolatry being expressed

Plate 1   **Raphael's drawing of Jonah,** from the drawing of Hosea and Jonah (ca. 1510). The Armand Hammer Collection. Image courtesy of the Board of Trustees, National Gallery of Art, Washington DC.

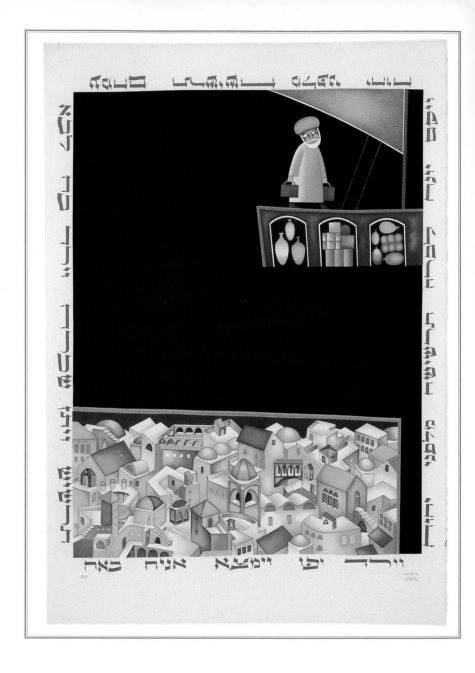

Plate 2   **David Sharir's _Jonah_** (1971). Reprinted by permission of Safrai Gallery, Jerusalem, Israel.

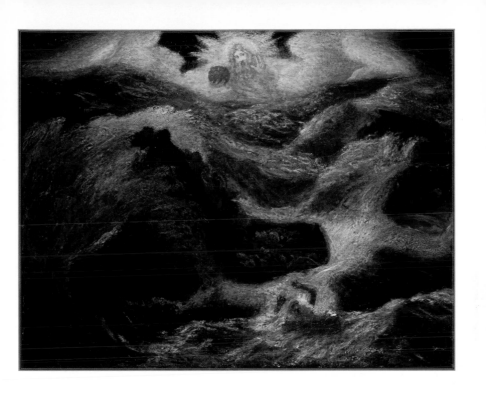

Plate 3   **Albert Pinkham Ryder's oil painting on canvas *Jonah*.** Reprinted by permission of Smithsonian American Art Museum, Washington DC / Art Resource, NY (ART25621).

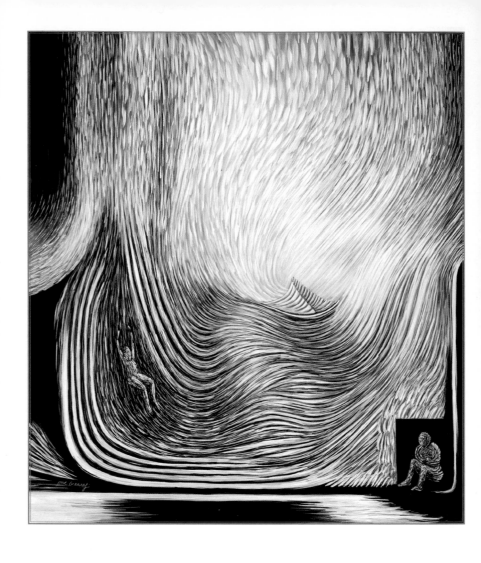

Plate 4 **Dennis McGeary's *Jonah***. Reprinted by permission of Dennis McGeary.

Plate 5   **Raphael and Lorenzetto's marble sculpture of Jonah** (ca. 1520). Designed and guided by Raphael, finished by Lorenzetto. Chigi Chapel, Church of Santa Maria del Popolo, Rome. Reprinted by permission of Santa Maria del Popolo, Rome / Mauro Magliani / SuperStock.

Plate 6   **Phillip Ratner's sculpture *Jonah*.** Reprinted by permission of the Dennis and
         Phillip Ratner Museum, Bethesda, MD.

Plate 7   **James Tissot's *Jonah***. Reprinted by permission of Jewish Museum, New York / SuperStock.

Plate 8   **Pieter Lastman's painting *Jonah and the Whale*** (1621). Reprinted by permission of SuperStock.

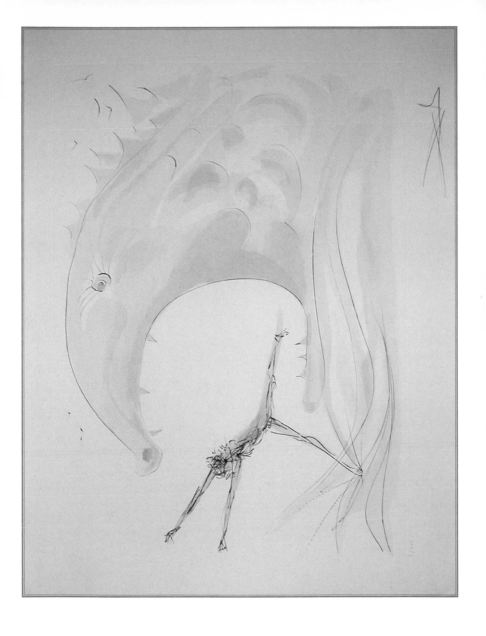

Plate 9 **Salvador Dali's *Jonah and the Whale*** (1975), one of 11 prints in the suite "Our Historical Heritage." © 2010 Salvador Dali, Gala-Salvador Dali Foundation / Artists Rights Society (ARS), New York. Image courtesy of Lockport Street Gallery, Plainfield, IL.

Plate 10 **Gerard Hoet's illustration *Jonah Entereth Nineveh*.** Image courtesy of History of Science Collections, University of Oklahoma Libraries. From Gerhard Hoet, *Figures de la Bible* (The Hague: Pierre de Hondt, 1728).

Plate 11   **Wayne Forte's painting *Lifeline: Jonah*** (2002). Reprinted by permission of Wayne Forte.

Plate 12 **Image of Jonah from marble sarcophagus from Italy** (ca. 290). Reprinted by permission of Holly Hayes / Sacred Destinations.

Plate 13 **Abraham van Linge's Jonah Window** (1630s). Christ Church Cathedral, Oxford. Reprinted by permission of Holly Hayes / Sacred Destinations.

Plate 14 **Eugen Spiro's *Jonah*.** In the "Prophetic Men" series. Reprinted by permission of SuperStock.

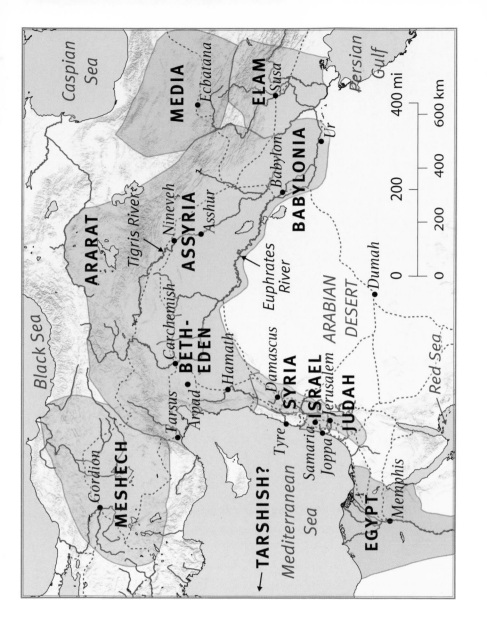

Plate 15   **The Setting of Jonah** (ca. 760 BC)

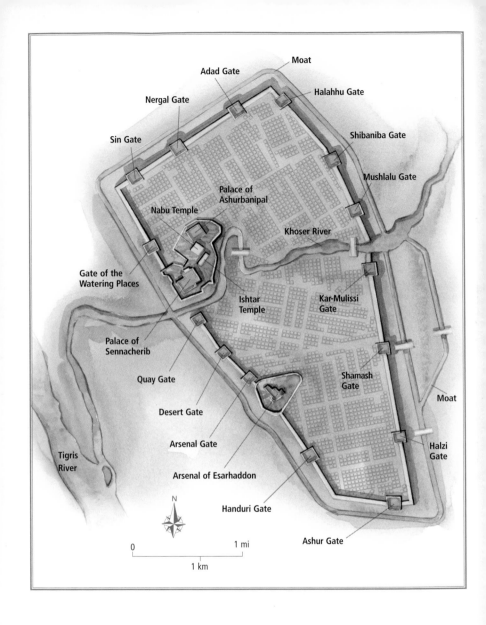

Plate 16　**The City of Nineveh** (ca. 1420–609 BC)

in his self-focused devotion to his well-being and comfort. And his situation points to the worthlessness of such idolatry. For all who cling to idols, the day eventually comes when it's as if we're sitting in oppressive heat under a useless, worm-withered shade tree.

Once more, God's question could be rendered as "Are you *right* to be angry for the plant?" *Jonah, is this really the wise and sensible response to the situation before you?* Toward Jonah, God's manner of speaking—like the words themselves and also God's actions—are ever gracious. In his question, we can hear him saying gently, "Stop it, Jonah." But Jonah's field of vision still extends no further than himself.

> And he said, "Yes, I do well to be angry, angry enough to die." (4:9)

For the third time in this brief series of verses, Jonah pronounces himself ready to call it quits on life. He doesn't grasp God's grace, and he doesn't trust God's ways. For Jonah, death offers more freedom than deference to God. Rather than give in to God, he wants to give up his earthly existence.

THE REAL ISSUE

The story's focus is tightening. On Jonah's part, everything's coming down to recurring anger and a death wish arising merely from his own personal discomfort and displeasure. And on God's part? He simply ignores Jonah's request for death. Instead he brings everything down to the issue of extending pity, compassion, and mercy to others.

> And the LORD said, "You pity the plant, for which you did not labor, nor did you make it grow, which came into being in a night and perished in a night." (4:10)

Jonah may be nodding his head. *Yes, of course. Isn't it tragic?* God continues:

> And should not I pity Nineveh, that great city, in which there are more than 120,000 persons who do not know their right hand from their left, and also much cattle? (4:11)

And that's it. *The end.* The story closes not with a happily-ever-after scene, but with an unanswered question from God to a tormented man. "We are left with a cliff hanger and must struggle to determine our own ending for the tale, to search our souls and see if we can view forgiveness as God does."[5] "The curtain falls," and the abrupt ending "leaves entirely open what the application of the story is."[6]

This unusual ending prompts us to do what God is leading Jonah to do—to compare God's heart with our own. Jonah's heart—for purely selfish reasons—is reacting with intense emotion about a single, short-lived plant whose growth and nurture he had nothing to do with. But God's heart is for a multitude of people whom he created, and who will live forever in eternity, either with God or in hell.

Who are these 120,000 persons God mentions who don't know right from left? Many think it most likely refers to Nineveh's small children; the number may be this large because "Nineveh" is understood to be the larger district that includes surrounding cities. Meanwhile, the final phrase in God's question—"and also much cattle"—might seem like a throwaway line. But it's packed with beauty, and it opens a wider window into God's heart and his plea for Jonah to finally understand it.

Once more, as so often in this book, we're reminded of words from David: "Man and beast you save, O LORD" (Ps. 36:6). We're also reminded of Jesus' words about our heavenly Father's concerned involvement even for a single sparrow falling to the ground (Matt. 10:29).

"Jonah had to understand," H. L. Ellison writes, "that the fulfillment of his wishes about Nineveh would have involved not only the destruction of innocent human beings but also of 'many cattle as well' that had become especially dependent on man."[7] As Douglas Stuart sums up, "God would have every right to spare Nineveh if only for the dumb animals in it!"[8]

FULL REDEMPTION

God's stated concern for the animals here is also a sneak peek at the size of redemption God has planned.

What is redemption? In the biggest sense, it's God's arrangement to reverse the curse of sin and to renew all things—to restore creation, not destroy it. God is on mission to reclaim and replenish his corrupted territory. "Behold," he says, "I am making *all things new*" (Rev. 21:5). God created both the physical and the spiritual, and he's going to redeem both the physical and the spiritual.

I'm convinced that for many Christians, their idea of redemption lines up more with ancient Greek philosophers than with what the Bible says. The ancient Greeks taught that it meant being rescued from the physical and the material, especially from our bodies. But God's idea is the rescue *of* the material, not rescue *from* the material. He's going to transform this present world into the world to come, so that voices in heaven shout, "The kingdom of the world has become the kingdom of our Lord and of his Christ" (Rev. 11:15). Likewise in the Lord's Prayer we see that God's ultimate goal is for earth to become like heaven—"Your kingdom come, your will be done, *on earth as it is in heaven*" (Matt. 6:10). His mission is to bring the culture of heaven to earth.

When it comes to this world's future, God will follow the same pattern he engineered in Noah's day, when he washed earth's surface clean of everything perverse and wicked but did not obliterate the planet. God isn't going to annihilate the world; instead, he's going to renew, redeem, and resurrect it through Christ.

That's why Christianity ultimately is not about isolated individuals "going to heaven," contrary to what many believe. That's not the Bible's primary storyline. God is up to something much bigger and much more tangible than that. He uses Christians to *bring heaven into this world*, transforming this broken world and making things right. God cares about the created order. Environmentalists make the mistake of turning the environment into a god, while Christians often make the mistake of thinking God doesn't care about the environment. Both perspectives miss the mark.

In Jesus, God is at work regaining, restoring, and extending all that Adam ruined and forfeited by his disobedience. Christianity is about Christ making everything sad come untrue, straightening out everything that's crooked, and correcting every injustice. As the second Adam (1 Cor. 15:46–47), Christ achieves for us no less than what the first Adam enjoyed, and much more. He came to succeed where the first Adam failed. We won't simply go back to the perfect garden; we'll enjoy a whole new incorruptible world.

God's closing remarks to Jonah about "much cattle" are a reminder that this world belongs to God, and he's in the process of gaining it all back, not giving it all up. Otherwise, those words about Nineveh's cattle don't make sense. For the Christian, and for all of creation, the best is yet to come—and knowing this truth makes all the difference. When we face the trials and temptations and fears that we'll inevitably encounter as fallen beings living in a broken world, this is the vision that will keep us pressing onward.

COMPASSIONATE CONDESCENSION

The Lord never stops showing his grace to Jonah. In this final scene, by sending and then killing the plant, and with his follow-up questions about it, he's stooping to Jonah's level for the moment. He's expressing things in Jonah's terms—"regard for what is useful and good . . . sorrow for its loss, unwillingness to see it perish. The higher moral ground is for the time abandoned. . . . But the lower ground is a step to the higher."⁹

With honest and careful reflection on Jonah's part, this questioning from God could help him escape himself and move forward into God's bigger, wider picture of a mission for the world. Will Jonah respond correctly? We don't know.

As is ultimately true in all our stories, so it is with Jonah's—*God gets the last word.* God has been intensely involved in Jonah's life to help him move beyond self-centeredness and answer this question: "Shouldn't I spare Nineveh?" It's a question, Stuart says, that every reader and hearer must reflect upon while pondering this story's message. "Anyone who replies 'Why is that such an important question?' has not understood the message. Anyone who replies 'No!' has not believed it."[10]

MISPLACED LOVE

Jonah doesn't understand the promiscuity of God's love. The fact that God's love is unconditionally deep and wide and offered to all people without distinction frustrates Jonah. But God comes back and essentially says, "You don't understand *my* love? I don't understand *yours!* Just look, Jonah—you value plants more than people!"

This stings—because we're all guilty of this in one way or another. One difference between God's love and our love is that God always values people most. Many of us have something we love more than people, be it sports, or cars, or money, or our business. Someone put it this way: in God's city, the inhabitants love people and walk on gold, while in man's city, the inhabitants love gold and walk on people.

God's deepest affections are reserved for people. In God's economy, people come before projects, not projects before people. God proves this not only in his reprieve for Nineveh but in continually pursuing Jonah.

TRIBAL OR MISSIONAL?

We can't escape a stark contrast in this story—the tribal mindset of Jonah versus the missional mindset of God. These two mindsets involve fundamentally different values. The highest value of a community with a tribal mindset is *self-preservation.* A tribal community exists solely for itself, and those within it keep asking, "How can we protect ourselves from those who are different from us?" A tribal mindset is marked by an unbalanced patriotism. It typically elevates personal and cultural preferences to absolute principles: *If everybody were more like us, this world would be a better place.*

But in a missional-minded community, the highest value isn't self-preservation but *self-sacrifice.* A missional community exists not primarily for itself but for others. It's a community willing to be inconvenienced and discomforted, willing to expend itself for others on God's behalf.

A tribal mindset is antithetical to the gospel. The gospel demands that we be missional, because the gospel is the story of God sacrificing himself for his enemies. Both these approaches are robustly present in Jonah's story. Jonah represents the best of a tribal mindset, the absolute best. He's like the trophy-boy for tribalism. And God—ever-gracious, ever-pursuing, ever-compassionate—carries the trophy for mission-mindedness.

Jonah runs *from* his enemies; God runs *toward* his enemies. Jonah serves himself; God serves the world.

WE'RE ALL TRIBAL

Here's the real tragedy: by nature, *we're all tribal,* in the root sense of being fundamentally self-centered. We're all convinced that if only everyone else was more like us, this world would enjoy smooth sailing. And because of that self-centeredness, our heart's default mode is self-preservation, not self-sacrifice. Our hearts naturally drift toward self-righteousness.

I've seen it again and again in counseling sessions with husbands and wives. For every couple I meet with, it starts out the same. First, fifteen minutes of the husband essentially saying, "If she were more like me, this marriage would be better." Then fifteen minutes of the wife essentially saying, "If he were more like me, this marriage would be better." In so many ways we're all that way, much more than we would like to admit. And for that to change, we need to be gripped by the missional heart of God.

GREAT FORGIVENESS, GREATER LOVE

Jonah's heart is stubborn, self-righteous, self-serving, and full of pride—such an utter contrast to God's gracious heart. Jonah really doesn't understand God's grace and therefore can't bring himself to trust him.

His anger over the wilted plant indicates Jonah's assumption that God is obligated to provide him with a comfortable life. After he's done what God asked him to do, after he's kept the rules, he's now thinking, *God owes me*. His thoughts are miles away from grace.

The great irony here is that Jonah emerges from this story as the chief antagonist. No one in this story deserves God's grace and mercy less; no one deserves God's anger more. Jonah is alive and well (despite his discomfort) only because God relented from fierce anger and extended him extravagant grace and mercy. Yet Jonah is furious with God for having shown this same mercy to the Ninevites.

When you've been forgiven as much as Jonah has, the right

response can never be anger with God but only love for him. Jonah should have been like the weeping woman who carried expensive ointment and knelt before Jesus and "began to wet his feet with her tears and wiped them with the hair of her head and kissed his feet and anointed them with the ointment" (Luke 7:38). Jesus therefore said, "Her sins, which are many, are forgiven—for she loved much. But he who is forgiven little, loves little" (7:47). Even if the Ninevites were such terribly worse sinners than Jonah was—which is highly debatable—God's forgiveness of their enormous sin would mean that much greater love for God in response, which is something Jonah should be rejoicing in.

Instead Jonah rejects what he sees God doing. His anger reveals that he still thinks the Ninevites aren't as deserving of God's good treatment as he is. He would actually rather die than yield to God's way of doing things. He's still choosing to place ultimate trust in what *he* thinks is best, not in what God says is best. And his refusal to understand and trust God's grace only stresses him out.

Jonah's anger is killing him. He's a miserable man because he's not free—he's still a slave to his own bitterness, limitations, and weaknesses. Some of us are miserable for the same reasons. God is working on us, teaching us to trust him—specifically in those areas where it's so very, very hard to discern what he's doing and why. And it hurts. Sometimes it's excruciatingly painful. He's telling us to let go of things we think we can't do without, things we believe make life worth living. He's pushing us, prodding us to give up our worthless idols, those things we've become so accustomed to that we actually think we can't live without them. We've depended on them so long that we're afraid to release them. They've come to actually define us. But they're actually enslaving us, and by holding onto them, we're blocking what God wants to give us. The pain we're experiencing is God's prying open our hands to take back all the gifts we're holding onto more tightly than to him.

FIRST AND LAST

As we saw earlier, self-reliance is the real slavery. When we place trust in ourselves, becoming our own gods, we forfeit the grace and the help that could be ours. So when Jesus said, "The last will be first, and the first last" (Matt. 20:16), he might even have worded it, "The Ninevites will be first, and Jonah last." Jerry Bridges applies this last-first, first-last principle to our own lives with these words: "If we are to succeed in living by grace, we must come to terms with the fact that God is sovereign in dispensing His gracious favors, and He owes us no explanation when His actions do not correspond with our system of merits."[11]

God owes no explanation to Jonah (or to us) for what he has done with the Ninevites. But in his overflowing grace, he works to help Jonah (and us!) to understand it all better. God is still coming after Jonah (and us!) to teach us more about his grace.

God never gives up on you. There's no one whose patience and forbearance toward you will ever be greater or longer-lasting than God's. Your wife or husband won't be this patient with you—your kids won't, your friends won't, your coworkers won't, your pastor won't. They'll all fail you at some point. You'll feel dehumanized, cheapened, discouraged, depressed, or radically disappointed by everyone and everything in this world.

But not by God. Nothing and no one will ever be as patient and forgiving toward you as God is. In all of existence, God is the only reality who refuses to give up on those he knows.

In unforgettable events and imagery, the story of Jonah reveals how this perfectly patient God pursues fugitives—a God who has every right to give up on rebels like us and to move on, but doesn't. It's a story that reveals forever the heart of God for sinners from every race, every age, and every social class.

PART THREE
NEVER-ENDING
SURPRISE

⚓

The Larger Scene
THE GOSPEL
ACCORDING TO JONAH

*But God, being rich in mercy . . . made us alive together
with Christ—by grace you have been saved.*

EPHESIANS 2:4–5

⚓

God likes to mix things up. At the very beginning of the
New Testament book of Hebrews, we read that when
God spoke "by the prophets" in Old Testament times,
he did so "at many times and *in many ways.*" How he spoke
through Jonah's story is certainly one of his most unusual ways
of addressing us. Jonah is the only prophetic book in the Bible
that focuses on the prophet himself rather than on his message.
Jonah's *life* is God's message to his people.

What is that message? God's message to his people through
the life of this prophet is that we're all like Jonah. We're all great
sinners—and God is a great Savior. Jonah's story is God's message of sin and grace, of desperation and deliverance. It's a message that reveals how quick we all are to run from God and how
quick God is to run after us. It's a message revealing that God's
capacity to forgive is greater than our capacity to sin; while our
sin reaches far, God's grace reaches farther. It's a message reveal-

ing the radical contrast between the sinful heart of mankind and the gracious heart of mankind's Creator.

THE BIG THREE

We've seen how the "giantesque" motif in the book of Jonah spotlights things that are large, things that are "great." As a storied presentation of the gospel, it especially reveals the expansiveness of three things—our sin, God's grace, and God's mission. There's nothing small about any of them.

This is important because our every tendency to ignore God is always a result of our downplaying the size and significance of our sin, of God's grace, and of God's mission. All our misgivings about God are the result of our not understanding the reach of our sin, the reach of God's grace, and the reach of God's mission. And if you're depending on anything except God to make your life worth living, it's because you're minimizing your sin, God's grace, and God's mission. You're in essence dismissing God.

It's not just atheists and agnostics and other non-Christians who write God off. Christians, too, can put him on the shelf. In fact, every time we sin, we're in that moment dismissing God. And it's always because in that moment we fail to understand the size of our sin, the size of God's grace, and the size of God's mission.

These three things also figure into our worship. As we looked at earlier, all of us are worshipers. Worship isn't simply something we do when we come to church and sing songs. Worship is so much bigger than that. It's the idea that every single one of us attributes ultimate worth to whatever we think will give our life meaning and make it worth living. In the words of G. K. Beale, "Whatever your heart clings to or relies on for ultimate security" is your object of worship.[1] If that's anything other than God—if we're depending on anything or anyone else to give our life meaning—then whether we're conscious of it or not, it's because we're minimizing our sin, minimizing God's grace, and minimizing God's mission.

THE EXPANSIVENESS OF OUR SIN

Except for God, everyone in this story—Jonah, each sailor, each Ninevite—is messed up. Jonah has his stubborn, prideful rebelliousness, the sailors have their worship of false gods, and the people of Nineveh have their "exceeding wickedness." They're all dysfunctional.

This reflects the fact that sin is no respecter of persons. It reaches to the religious and the irreligious, to the moral and the immoral, to the self-righteous and the unrighteous. It reaches those who think they're better than everyone and those who think they're worse.

Sin reached Jonah, who was part of God's community, the nation of Israel. Sin reached the sailors on that ship headed for Tarshish. Sin reached the Ninevites in their world-class metropolis. And sin reaches you and me. It hits all of us—not only *out there* but also *in here*. There's just as much sin inside the church as outside. And there's just as much sin for the man inside the fish's belly as for all those outside it.

It was easy for Jonah to despise the Ninevites for their perverse wickedness or to cry out in his psalm against the idolatrous. What he couldn't see was his own perverseness and idolatry. Jonah, as we've said, was like the prodigal's older brother, who thinks God owes him because he's kept all the rules.

But before we go too far in condemning Jonah's self-righteousness, we need to be aware of another (perhaps more subtle) side to self-righteousness that "younger brother" types need to be careful of. There's an equally dangerous form of self-righteousness that plagues the unconventional and the non-religious types. Anti-legalists can become just as guilty of legalism in the opposite direction. What do I mean? Those who are more like the younger brother—more irreligious—can easily take sinful pride in that fact.

Many younger evangelicals today are reacting to their parents' conservative, buttoned-down, rule-keeping flavor of "older brother religion" with a type of liberal, untucked, rule-breaking flavor of "younger brother irreligion." It screams out, "That's right! I *know* I don't have it all together, and you think you do; I *know* I'm not good, and you think you are. *And that makes me better than you!*" See the irony? We become self-righteous against the self-righteous.

Personally, I tend to resonate less with the rule keepers and more with the rule breakers—with those who have such a tough time staying on the narrow road. We're the kind who really love the gospel and God's grace because we feel our need so strongly; we know how desperate we are. But it's easy for us to feel a sense of superiority over all those upright-looking church people, whom we assume just don't really get the gospel.

I really like those passages where Jesus points his finger at the Pharisees. I want to stand right beside him and glare at each of those guys and shout, "That's right, buddy, don't look down your nasty nose at me!" If I did, I have a feeling Jesus might glare at me and say, as he did to Peter, "Get behind me, Satan! You are a hindrance to me. For you are not setting your mind on the things of God, but on the things of man" (Matt. 16:23). Self-righteousness goes in both directions. No matter what kind of person we are, it's always easier to detect sin and shortcomings and imperfections in other people than in ourselves.

Regardless of where each of us is on the self-righteousness continuum, we're all looking down our noses to some degree at someone who's unlike us. Our sin-corrupted survival mechanism makes us think, "I have to believe I'm better than *somebody.*" This rampant urge to maintain self-confidence and self-esteem is the default mode for fallen humanity. If we aren't better than *somebody,* we fear we'll lose all reason to live. It only shows that we're trying to trust in our superiority, rather than God's, in order to be saved.

The fact is, sin runs deep for all of us. If we're honest, each of us must confess what David did:

> I know my transgressions,
>   and my sin is ever before me. . . .
> Behold, I was brought forth in iniquity,
>   and in sin did my mother conceive me. (Ps. 51:3, 5)

David knows there was never a moment—going all the way back to the time of his conception—when he's been sin-free. *My entire personal history is marked by corruption.*

Our sin isn't merely some bad habit we've picked up along the way. It runs deep not only in *time* but also in *place.* David goes on to pray:

> Behold, you delight in truth *in the inward being,*
> and you teach me wisdom *in the secret heart.* (Ps. 51:6)

David knows that God's truth needs to invade the deepest places of our being. Why? Because sin invades the deepest places of our being.

That's what theologians are referring to when they speak of the doctrine of total depravity. They don't mean we're always as bad as we could possibly be. Thankfully, God's restraining grace keeps every single one of us—even the worst of us—from becoming utterly, unremittingly evil. Total depravity is rather the idea that sin has affected every part of our being—that there's no part of us that's entirely free of corruption and without need of God's intervention. And you and I will never fully own God's salvation if we don't first fully own our sin to that extent. Desperation always precedes deliverance. You'll never embrace the deliverance God offers if you don't first grasp how desperate you are.

Grief always precedes glory—always. The cross always precedes the crown—always.

THE EXPANSIVENESS OF GOD'S GRACE

God's grace is even more expansive than our sin. The whole story of Jonah is God's going after depraved, fallen fugitives.

We basically understand why God pursues Jonah, since he was a prophet and a part of God's people Israel, and he cared about God—at some level anyway. Jonah's prayer revealed that he was basically a friend of God, not an enemy.

Yet God also goes after Nineveh, as sinful a city as ever was. Jonah was pathetic in many ways, as we've seen, but Nineveh was violently wicked—perverse and sadistic. It makes me wonder why God didn't just send down fiery bolts of brimstone and do away with the whole nasty place. That would have seemed so much easier than the track this story takes. It would have spared God so much effort.

But the good news is that God's ability to clean things up is infinitely greater than our ability to mess things up. Yes, our sin reaches far in time and place, and to all types of people—moral, immoral, religious, irreligious. But God's grace reaches farther. God's grace is so massive, so expansive, so wide-ranging, that it tracks down both kinds of runners from God—those who try to rescue themselves by breaking the rules, and those who try by keeping them.

There's no place where you might be now, or where you might have been in the past, or where you might go in the future that will ever be beyond the reach of God's grace—nowhere.

Well, you may be thinking, *those words are fine for decent people, but Tullian, you don't know me and what I've done. You don't know my track record. You don't know the sins I keep falling into. You don't know how often I disregard God.* But God *does* know all that, and his pursuit of the Ninevites is the proof that his grace stretches to wherever you are. God's grace promises to give you a new beginning, a new purpose, a new destiny—if you'll stop running and allow him to set you free. If you allow him to pin you down, it will be the most magnificent defeat you've ever experienced.

The proof of God's expansive grace is the cross of Christ. And by virtue of what Christ accomplished on the cross, we're to further appropriate that grace and be killing sin in our lives—or it will be killing us.

How effective are we (those of us in the church) at proclaiming this expansive grace of the gospel of the cross of Christ? There's evidence to indicate we're doing badly—that our churches essentially attract only those who are already part of our "tribe," instead of reaching the full spectrum of people that the gospel is meant for. Consider these disturbing words from Tim Keller:

> Jesus' teaching consistently attracted the irreligious while offending the Bible-believing, religious people of his day. However, in the main, our churches today do not have this effect. The kind of outsiders Jesus attracted do not bother coming to our churches, even our most avant-garde ones. We tend to draw buttoned-down, moralistic people. The licentious and liberated or the broken and marginal avoid church. That can only mean one thing. If the preaching of our ministers and the practice of our parishioners do not have the same effect on people that Jesus had, then we must not be declaring the same message that Jesus did.[2]

Having examined Jonah's story, you may be inwardly congratulating yourself for not being like him. You may be telling yourself, "If I saw a huge wicked city repent, I know for sure I'd be thrilled about it—not angry like Jonah. And the other people in my church would feel just as excited about it as I would." But if your church is a great deal like the one Keller describes, then have you *really* learned the lesson of the book of Jonah about the expansive grace of God for everyone today?

THE EXPANSIVENESS OF GOD'S MISSION

God's gracious pursuit of Nineveh is also an unforgettable picture of the expansiveness of his mission. The Bible from cover to cover tells us that God is on a mission to transform this present world into the world to come. This tells us that God is interested in people of every tribe, tongue, and nation.

Ultimately, that was just as true in Old Testament times as in New Testament times. For centuries before Christ came, as the book of Jonah shows so vividly, his mission clearly extended beyond the bounds of Israel. It's in the New Testament, of course, that we see this come to explosive fruition, as Jew and Gentile come together in a magnificent way. But we also have glimpses and foreshadowings in the Old Testament of God's interest in all nations.

GOD IS NO RACIST

As I've said, to one degree or another, we all look down our noses at people who are different from us—those who dress differently, or look differently, or vote differently, or believe differently. Jonah had a national pride that caused him to look down on others, but we all have a personal pride that causes us to do the same. We all think our way is better than the way of others. Ultimately it's the same as racism.

But God is not a racist. His "nation," his "people," is open to everyone, without distinction. Jonah's story confirms the heart of God for people of every race, every background, every age, and every social status, which means this: just as sin and grace are no respecters of persons, so God's mission is no respecter of persons.

To me, the most startling aspect of God's mission is that he has called fallible people like you and me to take part in it. When Jesus came the first time, he began the process of "making all things new." When he comes a second time, he'll finish what he started. But in between those times, he has called *us* to carry on his mission.

God wants us to join him in his work of renewing peoples, places, and things. He wants Christians to renew their cultures to the honor and glory of God. God wants those he's redeemed to work at transforming this broken world and all its broken structures—families, churches, governments, businesses—in a way that reflects an answer to the Lord's Prayer: "Your kingdom come, your will be done, on earth as it is in heaven" (Matt. 6:10). We're to fill every aspect of the earth with the knowledge of God, our creator and redeemer. We've been redeemed by God to become agents of renewal.

In redeeming us, God doesn't simply rescue us from our sin; he also rescues us to do something—to develop the world around us to the glory of God. Therefore, when God saves us, we no longer have to settle for creating our own transitory meaning. How many of us spend our lives manufacturing our own reasons to live? Maybe it's raising our kids well so they'll turn out okay, and if they do, we'll think our life was worthwhile. There's so much talk about the need to leave a legacy. I'm not entirely sure what that means, but I don't like it. My life is not about leaving a legacy that makes people remember Tullian Tchividjian. God's mission for me and for all of us is so much bigger than that, which is liberating, because it means we don't have to try to manufacture our own passing legacy.

When God saves us, he gives us a new reason to live that's so much more significant than our fleeting legacies. We become part of an infinitely larger story than our personal history, larger even than the story of our family and nation. We no longer have to work for our own causes; instead we get to work for God's universal cause. That's a mission worth getting on board with!

God's mission and the direction it's going are so much bigger than our misconceptions. His mission is the one thing we can give our life to that will never be lacking in fulfillment and will never end.

When the great Russian novelist Leo Tolstoy faced his midlife crisis, he recorded his questions and thoughts in *A Confession*, and asked, "Is there any meaning in my life that the inevitable death awaiting me does not destroy?"[3] *God's mission is the right answer for that question for all of us.*

CONVERGENCE OF THE THREE

There's one place in human history where our sin, God's grace, and God's mission all converge. That place is the cross. That's where we see all three in their utmost clarity. We see an encumbrance of sin bearing down upon Christ, with such a horrible and toxic weight that it kills the God-man himself.

We also see God's grace at the cross. Christ is hanging there—bloodied, beaten, naked, and forsaken by his Father—*in our place*. It's *our sin* that we see on his shoulders. He's hanging there so that undeserving sinners will be granted unconditional acceptance. We see God's grace doing for us what we could never do for ourselves.

And we also see at the cross God's demonstration to reverse the curse of sin and to recreate all things. The cross is God's instrument that breaks down the stronghold of sin. At the cross and afterward, we see winter's grip loosened, and the snow begins to melt, and spring is in the air—Aslan is on the move. And you and I get to play a part in all that.

The gospel is the good news that in Jesus all things are made new. And our privilege is to receive and experience all this newness by faith in what Christ accomplished on the cross.

A CONTINUING REQUIREMENT

The story of Jonah shows us that this gospel of the cross—the good news that God relentlessly pursues sinners in order to rescue them—is just as much for Christians as it is for non-Christians. Jonah's life proves this, because Jonah, who knows God, obviously needs divine deliverance as much as anyone else in the story. In fact, his need for rescue gets far more emphasis than anyone else's. It's *his* destitution, not that of the Ninevites, that gets the most play. That alone should be enough to convince us that God's rescue is a continuing requirement for Christians and non-Christians alike.

The gospel isn't simply a set of truths that non-Christians must believe in order to become saved. It's a reality that Christians must daily embrace in order to experience being saved. The gospel not only saves us from the penalty of sin (justification), but it also saves us from the power of sin (sanctification) day after day. Or, as I once heard John Piper say, "The cross is not only a past place of objective substitution; it is a present place of subjective execution." Our daily sin requires God's daily grace—the grace that comes to us through the finished work of Jesus Christ.

Churches for years have struggled over whether their worship services ought to be geared toward Christians (to encourage and strengthen them) or non-Christians (to appeal to and win them). But this debate and the struggle over it are misguided. We're asking the wrong questions and making the wrong assumptions. The truth is that our worship services should be geared to *sinners in need of God's rescue*—and that includes both Christians and non-Christians. Since both groups need his deliverance, both need his gospel.

Christians need the gospel because our hearts are always prone to wander; we're always tempted to run from God. It takes the power of the gospel to direct us back to our first love. Consciously going to the gospel ought to be a daily reality and experience for us all. It means, as Jerry Bridges reminds us, "preaching the gospel to yourself every day."[4] We have to allow God to remind us every day through his Word of Christ's finished work on behalf of sinners in order to stay convinced that the gospel is relevant.

I find that I especially need a gospel refocus to help steer me away from a constant tendency to drift into a performance-driven relationship with God. I'm not alone in that tendency; Jerry Bridges observes how pervasive it is among us all:

> My observation of Christendom is that most of us tend to base our personal relationship with God on our performance instead of on His grace. If we've performed well—whatever "well" is in our opinion—then we expect God to bless us. If we haven't done so well, our expectations are reduced accordingly. In this sense, we live by works rather than by grace. We are saved by grace, but we are living by the "sweat" of our own performance.
>
> Moreover, we are always challenging ourselves and one another to "try harder." We seem to believe success in the

Christian life (however we define success) is basically up to us: our commitment, our discipline, and our zeal, with some help from God along the way. We give lip service to the attitude of the apostle Paul, "But by the grace of God I am what I am" (1 Corinthians 15:10), but our unspoken motto is, "God helps those who help themselves."

The realization that my daily relationship with God is based on the infinite merit of Christ instead of on my own performance is a very freeing and joyous experience.[5]

The difference between living for God and living for anything else is that when we live for anything else we do so to *gain* acceptance, but when we live for God we do so because we are *already* accepted. Real freedom (the freedom that only the gospel grants) is living for something because we already have favor instead of living for something in order to gain favor.

RICHES EVERY DAY

The gospel, as we've seen in Jonah, tracks down all runners— those who are in essence fleeing from God by trying on their own to be good (like so many inside the church), as well as those who flee God by living licentiously. Whichever direction we're running, we all need the gospel.

For me, this truth has been revolutionary. In studying and teaching this book of Jonah, there have been times when I've felt as if I'd become a Christian for the first time. God saved me when I was twenty-one, and that experience was genuine and effective—the deal was done. But I've come to see that I still need to experience the ongoing, liberating power of the gospel in a new way every day.

In particular, I've recognized this: the gospel shows us how to find two things in Christ that most of us long for more than anything else—*acceptance* and *affection*. I've discovered that God, in Jesus, has richly provided me with these two things—both of which I was created for, wired for, and designed to experience. They are, in fact, two fundamental marks of what it means to be human.

We spend our whole lives trying to gain them both, often without realizing it. Our deep, inescapable hunger for them both is behind so many of our daily pursuits.

ACCEPTANCE

The truth is that in Jesus, we have all the acceptance we long for. The gospel rescues us from the fear of being rejected. That fear looms large in all of us, though some have become quite sophisticated in trying to suppress and silence it.

We think our lives will become meaningful and worth living if we can just get in the right relationships with the right people, especially those who can help us reach where we want to go and get what we want to obtain, wherever and whatever that is. It could be the right level of income, or entry into the right social strata, or the right career, or the right marriage. If we can't make our dreams a reality, whatever they are, then life isn't worth living. We seek to gain that acceptance especially through our appearance, our achievements, or our performance.

In the movie *Rocky,* do you remember the scene on the night just before his big fight with Apollo Creed? Rocky knows he can't beat Creed; he tells his girlfriend, Adrian, "All I wanna do is go the distance" (something no other fighter has done with

Creed). If Rocky can somehow stay standing the full fifteen rounds, then he'll know for the first time in his life that he isn't "just another bum from the neighborhood."[6]

In my moments of gospel-disbelieving self-centeredness, there are certain things I look to so I'll know I'm not just another bum. I can't say what those might be for you, but I can tell you embarrassingly where my own heart wanders while looking for acceptance: *if my church grows, if my books sell, if there's harmony in my home, if my kids are loving and obedient and behaving well*—if I can just have those things, I tell myself, I'll feel the acceptance I long for, and my life will be worth living. That's when I have to be reminded of the truth: if we embrace what Christ has done on the cross for sinners, *we're in.*

In fact, all our desires for acceptance are really just pointers to what we *really* long for. They point to the one place, the one person, where we find real acceptance that can be experienced forever.

If you're a Christian, you're forever, unchangeably accepted by God, the only one who matters. When we grasp this, we realize that all those other things where we've searched for acceptance ultimately don't matter. They were never intended to be our saviors, our source of significance. They're too limited. All gods but God are too small.

No one can save us like Jesus can, yet we all look elsewhere for our functional saviors. We all do that, even those of us who say, "I believe Jesus is my Savior." We embrace that truth intellectually, but there are so many other things we look to daily, weekly, and monthly to provide us with the rescue, the meaning, the significance, and the acceptance we all long for.

Daily rescue happens as we continually reorient ourselves

to what Jesus has done for us. When we remind ourselves that Jesus came to reconcile sinners to God, and that as a result we now possess all the acceptance we need, it frees us from our slavery. It frees us from our idols. We no longer have to depend on those small things that will never be able to rescue us the way we long to be rescued. We become free of self-reliance and self-dependence.

AFFECTION

In Jesus, we also have all the affection we long for. The gospel rescues us from the fear of not being loved as well as our fear of loving.

We all long to be loved and also to love. Men especially can become relatively sophisticated at suppressing those longings, in large part because they believe such things aren't manly. And many women have been so hurt by someone in a past relationship that they now suppress their desire for love because trying to fulfill that desire is entirely too painful. Although our longing for love is such a fundamental part of our humanity, what we've discovered is that true love is downright dangerous. In *The Four Loves*, C. S. Lewis expresses this so insightfully:

> To love at all is to be vulnerable. Love anything, and your heart will certainly be wrung and possibly be broken. If you want to make sure of keeping it intact, you must give your heart to no one, not even to an animal. Wrap it carefully round with hobbies and little luxuries; avoid all entanglements; lock it up safe in the casket or coffin of your selfishness. But in that casket—safe, dark, motionless, airless—it will change. It will not be broken; it will become unbreakable, impenetrable,

irredeemable. . . . The only place outside Heaven where you can be perfectly safe from all the dangers and perturbations of love is Hell.[7]

Real love is risky. It opens us up to the possibility—even the likelihood—of intense emotional ache. So we suppress our longing for love and our willingness to love—which is why we all, to one degree or another, live clammed-up lives. Countless millions of people live in self-protective mode every day. They're afraid to love and to be loved because they're terrified of being taken. They're desperately afraid of getting trampled, since all of us, to one degree or another, have been trampled in the past.

This is why the world is such a cold place, so unfriendly. Our world lacks warmth because everyone's looking out for themselves. But no one *has* to live a clammed-up life. This is the glorious freedom that the ongoing power of the gospel can bring.

The gospel tells us first of all that we're forever loved by Jesus. In fact, if we embrace all that he has done for sinners, then we're assured that *absolutely nothing* "will be able to separate us from the love of God in Christ Jesus our Lord" (Rom. 8:39). Once we know that we're forever loved by Jesus, we're free to love others regardless of the risk, because our deep need to love will be satisfied.

A friend once told me, "My home is an unloving place." When he returned there every day from work, he said he wasn't loved the way he longed to be loved by his wife and kids. I listened to him, and we talked further. Eventually I responded, "Maybe, just maybe, you're looking at this from the wrong perspective." I suggested that for six months he ask himself the following question each day when he came home from work:

"Who here can I love? Who here needs my love right now?" I told him to pray about this before he walked in the door, asking God to show him the answer to that question. This man did that, and things at home changed, at least for a while.

Unfortunately, the fear that our love toward others will not be reciprocated is something that paralyzes many of us. It prevents parents from properly loving their kids, and husbands and wives from properly loving each other. We come to this conclusion: *I will love you only to the degree that you love me.* It's an attitude that enslaves us. But the gospel frees us from that.

I too enjoy receiving love from my family. I'm ecstatic when my kids love me and express affection toward me. Something in me comes alive when they do that. But I've learned this freeing truth: I don't *need* that love, because in Jesus, I receive all the love I need. This in turn enables me to *love my kids without fear or reservation.* I get to revel in their enjoyment of my love without needing anything from them in return. I get love *from* Jesus so that I can give love *to* them.

The gospel tells us that God in Christ loved us *a lot*—even while we hated him. Fully realizing this will pave the way for us to love others unconditionally as well. We realize and experience this liberating truth: "By this we know love, that he laid down his life for us, and we ought to lay down our lives for the brothers" (1 John 3:16). This kind of lay-down-your-life love is the clearest indicator of a gospel-centered life.

But laying down your life for others is impossible. It's too *scary*—unless you know you've been eternally loved by Christ. Then you're free to give your life to others, because you've received so much yourself.

Do you realize how radically different this world would be

if that was the rule instead of the exception in all our relation-ships? The most powerful way we can join God on his mission to bring heaven to earth—to warm this place up, and renew and redeem and fix this broken planet—is by applying the gospel in this way, in all our relationships. Just try it for six months and see what happens.

The Later Scenes
SOMETHING GREATER
THAN JONAH

Be merciful, even as your Father is merciful.
JESUS, IN LUKE 6:36

⚓

As Jonah's story ends, we wonder: What happens later with this guy? And what happens later with Nineveh? It's easier to answer the second question than the first.

A QUICK RISE

We know from history that immediately after Jonah's time, the Assyrians launched their greatest era of expansion and power, becoming the mightiest empire the world had ever witnessed. Nineveh, already "exceedingly great" in Jonah's time, became far greater—in power and prestige, as well as in appearance. It became "one of the architectural wonders of the world."[1] Nineveh also became far richer, by way of the plunder from Assyria's conquests. A later biblical prophet would say of her, "There is no end of the treasure or of the wealth of all precious things" (Nah. 2:9).

Assyria's reach expanded in a huge arc from the Persian

Gulf and Babylon through the upper reaches of the Tigris and Euphrates valleys, then down along the eastern Mediterranean coast. By 722 BC, only a generation after Jonah, the Assyrians conquered the northern kingdom of Israel. Israel's northern border, which had been strengthened according to the God-guided prophecy of Jonah back in his younger days, was shattered. The hills of Galilee where Jonah had grown up became the property of a foreign power.

Israel's final king, Hoshea, paid tribute to Assyria at first, then conspired against Assyrian dominance. His rebellion was quickly dealt with. Samaria, Israel's capital, was besieged and breached, and her people deported. "In the ninth year of Hoshea, the king of Assyria captured Samaria, and he carried the Israelites away to Assyria" (2 Kings 17:6).

All this was an act of God's judgment, as his Word carefully explains:

> This occurred because the people of Israel had sinned against the LORD their God . . . and had feared other gods. . . . And they did wicked things, provoking the LORD to anger, and they served idols, of which the LORD had said to them, "You shall not do this." (2 Kings 17:7–12)

To use the words from Jonah's psalm from inside the great fish, Israel was "paying regard to vain idols"—which meant they would thereby "forsake their hope of steadfast love" from the Lord (Jonah 2:8).

God had warned them that disaster was coming. But unlike the Ninevites in Jonah's day, the Israelites did not repent:

The LORD warned Israel . . . by every prophet and every seer, saying, "Turn from your evil ways. . . ." But they would not listen, but were stubborn, as their fathers had been, who did not believe in the LORD their God. (2 Kings 17:13–14)

Jonah had hoped to see divine judgment fall against Nineveh; it fell instead against Jonah's homeland:

Therefore the LORD was very angry with Israel and removed them out of his sight. None was left but the tribe of Judah only. . . . And the LORD rejected all the descendants of Israel and afflicted them and gave them into the hand of plunderers, until he had cast them out of his sight. . . . So Israel was exiled from their own land to Assyria until this day. (2 Kings 17:18–23)

Meanwhile, for the people of God still left in the southern kingdom of Judah, Assyria's continuing escalation in power would make the story of God's compassionate deliverance of Nineveh back in Jonah's time even more shocking to their ears.

This gives us much to think about. Since God, in the days of Jonah, displayed such compassion for Nineveh—a future rod of his wrath against his own people—then how great must be his compassion for our great cities today, even in their corruption and depravity. May our own hearts share in that compassion with him.

A QUICK FALL

Assyria continued its expansion after Israel's fall, pressing southward clear to the heart of Egypt. But the newer generations of

Assyrians didn't follow the example of Nineveh's repentance in Jonah's day. And God took notice. Through the prophet Nahum in Judah (now a vassal state under Assyria's dominance), the Lord declared what he observed. Nineveh was "the bloody city, all full of lies and plunder"; the many lands she conquered had to suffer her "unceasing evil" (Nah. 3:1, 19).

In chilling words, God pronounced Nineveh's verdict and sentence: "I will make your grave, for you are vile" (Nah. 1:14). Nineveh's fate would be "desolation and ruin!" (2:10). She would be "utterly cut off" and "wasted" (1:15; 3:7).

In the middle of the seventh century, only a few generations after Jonah, Assyria suddenly began to weaken. Her decline quickly accelerated. Her once-vanquished enemies now sprang on her. Her borders collapsed. A force of Babylonians, Medes, and Scythians rushed to Nineveh and captured the great city. Assyria's king died in the flames of her destruction. Before the end of the seventh century, Nineveh was a heap of ruins, never to rise again.

PROPHETIC ECHOES

Although Jonah's story is unique among the prophetic books in being more about the man than his words, there's a lot about Jonah's message that is echoed and reinforced in the prophetic books that follow—during those centuries when successive empires were rising and falling in the ancient Near East.

The repentance that wicked Nineveh demonstrated so quickly and resolutely and wholeheartedly is something that God, speaking later through his prophets, will implore from his own people. Essentially, God's message to both Nineveh and to his own people was the same: *Repent!* But his message to Israel and Judah is far more profound and multifaceted than the terse doom Jonah had announced: "Yet forty days, and Nineveh shall be overthrown!" (Jonah 3:4).

God's message to his own people through his prophets included not only warnings and indignation, but also grief and the pleadings of his loving heart. Often his tone and manner of speaking show the same graciousness that God kept showing to Jonah. We hear it when he says through Isaiah, "Come now, let us reason together," and then calls for the same action the Ninevites had exhibited long before:

> Wash yourselves; make yourselves clean;
>> remove the evil of your deeds from before my eyes;
> cease to do evil,
>> learn to do good;
> seek justice,
>> correct oppression. (Isa. 1:16–18)

Later, when God sends Jeremiah into a potter's house, he uses the image of a potter and his clay to illustrate his absolute and exclusive right to select the objects of his mercy—the very right he had exercised so freely and surprisingly in Nineveh. In fact, the example of Nineveh may have come blazing into Jeremiah's mind as God speaks to him these words:

> If at any time I declare concerning a nation or a kingdom, that I will pluck up and break down and destroy it, and if that nation, concerning which I have spoken, turns from its evil, *I will relent of the disaster that I intended to do to it.* (Jer. 18:7–8)

Here was a fresh reminder of the sovereign principle God had asserted to Moses on Mount Sinai: "I will be gracious to whom I will be gracious, and will show mercy on whom I will show mercy" (Ex. 33:19)—a principle that Jonah should have taken to heart.

This is essentially the same point Jesus makes in his parable of the vineyard laborers. Some were hired much later in the day than others, yet all received equal pay at the workday's end. When those who toiled the longest protested, the boss's reply expresses the attitude of God himself whenever we (like Jonah) question God's allocation of his grace and mercy: "Am I not allowed to do what I choose with what belongs to me?" (Matt. 20:15).

REMEMBER NINEVEH

Links with Jonah to other prophets are especially strong in the brief writings of the prophet Joel.[2] The parallels are striking and instructive, leading us to think that once again, God wants his people to keep the story of Nineveh's deliverance in their active memory.

The disaster from God that Joel pictures is that of successive waves of all-devouring locusts. Joel doesn't announce a forty-day period before God's wrath will fall, as Jonah did to the Ninevites, but the deadline is coming soon enough:

> Alas for the day! For the day of the LORD *is near,*
> and as destruction from the Almighty it comes. (Joel 1:15)

Just as Nineveh's king did, Joel calls for repentance, sackcloth, and fasting (Joel 1:13–14; 2:12). As food disappears, the livestock groan (1:18), just as they did in Nineveh's enforced fast. The "Who knows?" question that Nineveh's king asked about God's ways is also asked by Joel:

> Who knows whether he will not turn and relent,
>   and leave a blessing behind him? (Joel 2:14)

Joel even cites the same ancient biblical truths about God's character that Jonah had cherished: "Return to the LORD your God, for he is gracious and merciful, slow to anger, and abounding in steadfast love; and he relents over disaster" (Joel 2:13).

Perhaps with these echoes from Jonah's story, God wants his people to think and say to each other, "Remember how completely the Ninevites repented? Remember how God completely delivered them? Let's do the same—and trust God to respond the same way for us."

But repentance on the scale of Nineveh's was never repeated among God's people in the Promised Land. Therefore, less than a century and a half after the northern kingdom was conquered and sent into exile by Assyria, the southern kingdom of Judah suffered the same fate at the hands of the Babylonians.

JONAH'S FUTURE

And what about Jonah? Did he finally learn his lesson? Did he finally figure out God's grace? Perhaps he did, as the very existence of the book of Jonah might attest. Jonah himself is very possibly the book's sole author, as many believe; he had to be at least a major source for it, since so much of it tells what only he would have known about (such as his experience inside the fish and his conversations with God outside Nineveh). Even elements in the story that were outside Jonah's immediate observation could have been picked up by him later. For example, Douglas Stuart explains how Jonah could have learned about the sacrifices and vows the sailors offered after throwing Jonah overboard:

> As a significant Northern prophet, Jonah was hardly an obscure personage. News of his rescue at sea, his trip to Nineveh, and his eventual return would surely have spread widely in his later years, possibly occasioning a meeting between one or more of the sailors and Jonah. In fact, if they heard that Jonah were actually alive, one wonders how the sailors could have failed to search him out.[3]

One argument sometimes made against Jonah's authorship of the book is the negative light in which Jonah is portrayed. As one commentary notes, "Jonah's public image does not fare at all well in the book. Where else in the Scriptures (or any ancient literature, for that matter) does an author of a narrative so thoroughly deprecate himself or herself?"[4]

But if Jonah truly learned his lesson from God—especially as he reflected more deeply on it in the months and years to come—what better way to publicly acknowledge his wrong actions and attitudes than to write the story in the exact form we have it today? In fact, if he *hadn't* learned his lesson from God, why would he give others his inside information on all this, allowing *them* to write such an unflattering account of him?

Perhaps Jonah's ability to record the story in this form was a true gift from God—yet another mark of his amazing mercy.

In this way, God would have rescued Jonah far more profoundly than even Jonah's fish-belly psalm acknowledged.

Jonah gets no glory in this book; God gets it all. Isn't that the way a humbled prophet would want it? (Isn't that, in fact, the very reason we all exist—to glorify God and enjoy him forever?)

With this in mind, we can imagine the repentant prophet writing down the story, limiting it to the barest of details, and leaving out anything that might be seen as self-justifying in any way. He sticks with the essential facts—his terrible disobedience, absurdly carried out; his rescue through God's massive, miraculous intervention; his outward obedience after God gave him a second chance; the spectacularly unprecedented results in Nineveh as God used him; his own shamefully narrow and selfish reaction; and finally, God's corrective actions and tender questioning to show him his error.

Even though the story adheres to these basic facts, it has a depth that satisfies. It isn't shallow and sentimental, but has the rich texture added by mysteries and unanswered questions. Perhaps God's gifts to Jonah included not only the grace to finally repent, but the grace to be such a skillful writer of his own story.

A SCARRED MAN

In a lengthy three-part poem about Jonah,[5] John Piper takes us for a visit to the prophet forty years later. The prophet is gray-bearded, with a scar across his cheek. He's a "legend in the land," and his evenings are spent speaking with young aspiring prophets who gather in his garden to question and learn from him.

In Piper's poem, an inquisitive young lad named Hosea—the

future prophet Hosea in the Bible—is there in the garden one night, and asks about the scar. Jonah tells his story and explains how the scar came from a "razor tooth" in the great fish's mouth, when it vomited him out onto dry land. He refers to the scar as a "sweet sign of grace." The old man also, with tears, confesses his rebellion against God:

> . . . I knew that he
> Was good. And that he did not see
> Me as his enemy. But when
> Unholy hatred rises, then
> A man must either die beneath
> The weight of conscience and the teeth
> Of truth, or by some fatal act
> Of treason, sign a deadly pact
> With blind absurdity, and make
> A foe out of his God, and take
> The wings of feigned escape to fly
> As far from God as such a lie
> Will let him fly, and there be found,
> Or die.

To the young Hosea, Jonah relates philosophically the utter surprise of his encounter in the fish, and what it did for him.

> . . . the path to life is strange,
> And none can know the kind, or range
> Of deaths that one must die along
> The way that leads to life. The song
> That satisfies the human soul,
> When nothing tender can console,
> Is learned beside the grave, or from
> Within.

He says the experience inside the fish was, sadly, not enough at the time to help him "see and savor" God's truth—because "sin is deep," and "I was so slow to learn."

A SIN-STAINED LEGACY

In Piper's poem, Jonah tells Hosea that after God delivered Nineveh, he stayed and observed the city, feeling his own pain:

> . . . day by day I watched God bless
> A pagan people by his grace.
> And every day I touched my face,
> And ran my finger on this scar
> And felt with shameful fire: how far
> I'd fallen from the mercy that
> It meant.

He acknowledges that the judgment he'd wanted God to rain down on Nineveh was essentially rained down on him instead. And the result, Jonah now knows, is that his legacy will be the story of his own sinfulness rather than the lessons he learned only later:

> The fame
> That I will have, young man, in years
> To come, will not be for my tears
> Of sorrow over how much pain
> It took to purge the ugly stain
> Of hate out of my callous soul.
> I am a different man. The bowl
> Of wrath I would have poured on that
> Great city, God did make a vat
> Of boiling mercy for my sin,

And cast me into it. And in
That fierce and cleansing clemency,
At last, did make me feel and see
His ways, which are as high above
My own as is the flying dove
Above the crawling snake. But I . . .
Will be remembered for a slow
And stubborn heart, and I will go
Down into history still hard
And murmuring at grace, and marred
With bitterness, in spite of all
God's sweet affliction of my gall.

Though we today indeed remember Jonah for his stubborn sin, his story points us steadily beyond that to God's great mercy.

THE SWALLOWABLE LITTLE MAN

Others have imagined Jonah's life beyond Nineveh in a more humorous and fantastic vein.

Robert Frost, America's grand old man of poetry in the twentieth century, occasionally explored God and faith in his earlier poems. Then, entering his seventies after a decade of great personal loss—his wife's death, the death of one of his daughters shortly after childbirth, and the suicide of another—Frost wrote two poetic dramas filled with references to God. The first, *A Masque of Reason*, is based on Job's story of suffering and comes across as rather inconclusive. But the second, *A Masque of Mercy*, has Jonah as the main character and wraps up in a more aesthetically pleasing way.[6] In creative uniqueness it tackles the conflict in Jonah's thinking, as it "explores the ancient riddle of how God can be just and also be merciful."[7] It also pulls Jonah toward Christ and the cross.

The brief play is set late on a stormy night inside a modern bookstore run by someone named Keeper, a pagan skeptic who'll later say, "I'd rather be lost in the woods than found in church." His alcohol-loving wife, Jesse Bel, is more openly searching for faith and sees that longing in others around her as well: "The world seems crying out for a Messiah," she'll say.

The play begins with Keeper and Jesse Bel locking their shop's door for the evening, leaving inside a customer named Paul (as it turns out, it's *the* Paul—the apostle). But someone bangs at the locked door. As they reluctantly let him in, the harried stranger exclaims, "God's after me!"

"You mean the Devil is," Jesse Bel remarks.

"No, God."

"I never heard of such a thing," she protests.

The fugitive answers, "Haven't you heard of Thompson's 'Hound of Heaven'?"

Paul at once interjects by quoting the familiar opening lines: "I fled Him, down the nights and down the days; I fled Him, down the arches of the years."

But Keeper grumbles at the fugitive: "This is a bookstore—not a sanctuary."

From this strange and amusing start, the play proceeds to an extended conversation that keeps coming back to God.

"Why is God after you?" Keeper asks. "To save your soul?"

"No," the fugitive replies. He tells them he's a prophet and that his name is Jonah. He's been sent seven times "to prophesy against the city evil."

"What have you got against the city?" Keeper asks.

"*He* knows," Jonah answers. God knows.

Jonah identifies himself further (though Paul has already caught on): "I'm in the Bible, all done out in story." Then he complains, "*I can't trust God to be unmerciful.*"

Paul responds, "There you have the beginning of all wisdom."

Jonah tells them about his earlier flight from God, and the storm, and the boat, and the crew—and the whale.

Jesse Bel sympathizes: "You poor, poor swallowable little man."

But Paul recognizes a man who needs rescue. He goes up to Jonah and crosses his forearms—to illustrate *the* cross.

"What good is that?" Jonah asks.

Jonah tells these three that he would like to announce an earthquake to destroy "the city evil," but he's sure God wouldn't send it. "Nothing would happen," he says—but suddenly a tremor sends books crashing from the store's shelves. Meanwhile, Jonah keeps hearing noises that he suspects are from God in pursuit of him.

Paul asks Jonah what he wants to see in God, if not mercy.

Justice is Jonah's answer; justice "before all else."

GETTING GOD WRONG

Throughout Frost's play, Jonah wrestles with how God doesn't seem to live up to justice. Jonah has been taught that people should be "strong, careful, thrifty, diligent," and he's upset by God's "modern tendency" not to punish those who fail to measure up to those ideals.

The conversation inside the bookshop bounces around in

history, philosophy, and theology, and finally returns to mercy. Paul directs everyone's attention to the Sermon on the Mount and the "beautiful impossibility" it portrays:

> An end you can't by any means achieve,
> And yet can't turn your back on or ignore,
> That is the mystery you must accept.

It throws us by necessity onto mercy. "Mercy is only to the undeserving," Paul says, which includes all of us, in God's sight:

> Here we all fail together, dwarfed and poor.
> Failure is failure, but success is failure.
> There is no better way of having it.

A door opens on its own to the store's cellar. Paul, who has had a cross painted on the cellar's ceiling, encourages Jonah to go down into its dark depths: "You must make your descent like everyone." It will require Jonah's abandonment and submission, essentially a yielding of self.

Jonah is hesitant. Finally he steps to the threshold, but the door slams in his face, knocking him to the floor. Lying there, collapsed and fading out, he confesses, "I think I may have got God wrong entirely." His own sense of justice, he says, "was about all there ever was to me." His last words are these: "Mercy on me for having thought I knew."

Kneeling over him, Paul speaks his own concluding words, affirming that "the best we have to offer" isn't enough. "Our very best, our lives laid down like Jonah's . . . may not be found acceptable in Heaven's sight."

The play closes with words from Keeper, who admits,

"My failure is no different from Jonah's." He says they should lift Jonah's body and lay him "before the cross," just as Paul wanted. As the curtain falls, Keeper moves toward the prostrate Jonah and offers the play's final line:

Nothing can make injustice just but mercy.

Or as the New Testament says, "Mercy triumphs over judgment" (James 2:13).

Those writers who, like Piper, Frost, and others, engage seriously with Jonah's life and message always seem to come back to the mystery of God's mercy. It's a conclusion that Paul (the real apostle, not the one in Frost's play) arrived at after laying out the gospel in the book of Romans: "For God has consigned all to disobedience, *that he may have mercy on all*" (Rom. 11:32). That fact lifted Paul immediately into a surge of astonishment and praise: "Oh, the depth of the riches and wisdom and knowledge of God! How unsearchable are his judgments and how inscrutable his ways!" (11:33). And that in turn prompted a call for every believer's rightful response: "I appeal to you therefore, brothers, *by the mercies of God,* to present your bodies as a living sacrifice" (12:1).

This bottom-line focus on God is why any speculation about Jonah's post-Nineveh experiences, as well as the search for more psychological details behind his actions and words in this story, are relatively unimportant. Douglas Stuart helps us see this:

"What is God really like?" is thus a more important question in this book than the question "What was Jonah really like?"

About the latter question one may speculate; about the former question the book leaves no doubt.[8]

In the end, this story is not so much the book of Jonah, but a book of God.

LAST WORD

Jonah, you'll remember, was first mentioned in the Bible in 2 Kings in a narrative about his success as a prophet in Israel, used by God to help strengthen his homeland. When we next see him in the book of Jonah, it's a drastically different situation, as that book closes with an angry, frustrated prophet facing God's gracious interrogation. Finally, the Bible's last word on Jonah comes in the Gospels, from the lips of Jesus. He connects this prophet to himself while speaking words of warning to the religious leaders of his day.

Twice in Matthew, and once in Luke, we see those religious leaders coming to Jesus, asking for a sign. They were asking from wrong hearts and wrong motives. Jesus therefore calls them "an evil and adulterous generation" (Matt. 12:39). So instead of performing an on-the-spot, on-demand miracle for them, he points them back to God's Word. The sign they will get is already written there.

Many Old Testament prophets said and did many things that pointed to Jesus, and these can legitimately be called "signs." But Jesus—for this crowd—names just *one* prophet as *the* sign of himself: Jonah, of all people! Jonah, lodged for days in a great fish's belly—"So will the Son of Man be three days and three nights in the heart of the earth" (Matt. 12:40). Jesus' later resurrection would make all this clear, a picture packed with significance and encouragement for his disciples down through the ages.

Jesus also declares to the religious leaders that the Ninevites of Jonah's time will be heard from again someday. In eternity, in the coming hour of judgment, these Ninevites will rise and condemn those people who stand there watching and listening to Jesus with selfish, judgmental hearts. But on that future day, they'll hear their condemnation announced not only from the mouth of God, but from the mouths of ancient, arrogant, idolatrous pagans from a foreign power who by God's grace were humbled, rescued, and reformed.

Jesus isn't saying the people of Nineveh were inherently better than the people in Israel of his own day. No, each group represents an "evil and adulterous generation." But the difference is this: the Ninevites genuinely repented; most of the people of Israel in Jesus' day never would.

And while the Ninevites repented at words spoken by a disaster-prone, severely reluctant prophet with a diseased heart, the people in Jesus' day are getting God's words from a bigger, better, deeper, richer, fuller source. They're hearing God's words from *God in the flesh*—right here before their eyes. "*Something greater than Jonah is here*" (Matt. 12:41). What possible excuse can they have for not repenting? Or can we?

ANOTHER MESSENGER

In sending Jonah as his messenger to sinful Nineveh, God showed his boundless grace and faithfulness.

But centuries later, God sent another messenger to sinful mankind. Only this messenger went willingly and joyfully because he knew the heart of God. In fact, he *was* the heart of God. He would be called "the Word" because he himself was God's message. He was everything God wanted to say to the world—all wrapped up in a person.

Instead of fleeing from God's call in rebellion and running away from his enemies, this new messenger ran *toward* his enemies, in full submission to his Father's will, despite what it would cost him. For "we were enemies" of God (Rom. 5:10)—all of us—so much so that we rejected and crucified his Son.

Fully knowing that this death was his destiny, this new messenger nevertheless pursued God's rescue mission with a totally engaged heart. "For the joy that was set before him," the Bible tells us, he "endured the cross" (Heb. 12:2) so that God's enemies, you and I, could become God's friends.

Like Jonah thrown overboard, this new messenger would be a sacrifice, with the result that others were saved. This new messenger, like Jonah, would spend three days in utter darkness. But unlike Jonah, he would emerge with wholehearted determination to pursue his enemies with life-giving love. He went on this mission because he wanted to—not because he had to.

When God's mercy was shown to Jonah and to his enemies, Jonah was intensely angered. But this new messenger was the happy extension of God's grace toward his enemies—not angry and embittered, but "anointed . . . with the oil of gladness" (Heb. 1:9). Jonah is all about self-protection; this new messenger is all about joyful self-sacrifice. No wonder Jesus says that he is "greater than Jonah"! Jesus is the greater-than-Jonah who succeeded where Jonah failed.

Yes, Jesus is all over this story of Jonah. And as we truly see him there, we'll appreciate him all the more each time we listen to him in the Gospels, where, if our eyes and hearts are open wide, we'll find ourselves more surprised than ever.

TO WALK IN FREEDOM

There's a story told, from Civil War days before America's slaves were freed, about a northerner who went to a slave auction and purchased a young slave girl. As they walked away from the auction, the man turned to the girl and told her, "You're free."

With amazement she responded, "You mean, I'm free to do whatever I want?"

"Yes," he said.

"And to say whatever I want to say?"

"Yes, anything."

"And to be whatever I want to be?"

"Yep."

"And even go wherever I want to go?"

"Yes," he answered with a smile. "You're free to go wherever you'd like."

She looked at him intently and replied, "Then I will go with you."

Jesus has come to the slave market. He came to us there because we could not go to him. He came and purchased us with his blood so we would no longer be a slave to sin but a slave to Christ, which is the essence of freedom.

And now there's no freer place to be in life than *going with him*—with the One who is himself our true liberty.

NOTES

A CURE FOR GOSPEL CONFUSION

1. *The New Geneva Study Bible*, ed. R. C. Sproul (Nashville, TN: Nelson, 1995), 1417.
2. Ray Stedman, from his sermon "Jonah: The Reluctant Ambassador," Peninsula Bible Church, Palo Alto, CA (May 22, 1966).
3. Janet Howe Gaines, *Forgiveness in a Wounded World: Jonah's Dilemma* (Atlanta: Society of Biblical Literature, 2003), 8.
4. Martin Luther, *Table Talk*, trans. William Hazlitt (Philadelphia: The Lutheran Publication Society, 1857), sec. DXLVII.
5. Matt. 12:38–42; 16:1–4. See also Luke 11:29–32.
6. Fred S. Kleiner, *Gardner's Art through the Ages: A Global History*, 13th ed. (Florence, KY: Cengage Learning EMEA, 2008), 293.
7. Ibid., 292.
8. Augustine, "Letter to Deogratias," in *Letters,* vol. 2 (Washington DC: Catholic University of America Press, 1953), 170.

THE STORY'S BEGINNING

1. Lloyd John Ogilvie, *God's Best for My Life* (Eugene, OR: Harvest, 1981), daily reading for November 13.
2. Raphael's combined drawing of the prophets Hosea and Jonah (c. 1510) is in the Armand Hammer collection of master drawings, National Gallery of Art, Washington DC.
3. John Calvin, *Commentaries on the Twelve Minor Prophets*, trans. John Owen; from comments on Jonah 1:1–2.
4. Ibid.
5. Frank Dumont, "De Gospel Raft" (1878), in *Minstrel Songs, Old and New* (Boston: Oliver Ditson, 1883), 176–77; http://www.pdmusic.org/1800s/78dgr.txt (accessed April 25, 2009).
6. H. L. Ellison, *Jonah*, Expositor's Bible Commentary (EBC), vol. 7 (Grand Rapids, MI: Zondervan, 1985), 363.
7. Calvin, *Commentaries,* Jonah 1:3.
8. Ibid.
9. G. K. Chesterton, "The Miracle of Moon Crescent," in *The Incredulity of Father Brown* (1926; repr. New York: Penguin, 1958), 94.
10. "For what does the term 'old covenant' imply but the concealing of the new? And what does the term 'new covenant' imply but the revealing of the old?" Augustine, *City of God*, Great Books of the Western World, vol. 16, trans. Marcus Dods (Chicago: University of Chicago Press, 1990), 501.

SCENE 1

1. David Sharir's 1971 portrait of Jonah aboard ship is in the Safrai Gallery in Jerusalem.
2. From chaps. 7–9 in Herman Melville's *Moby Dick* (1851).

3. H. L. Ellison, *Jonah*, Expositor's Bible Commentary (EBC), vol. 7 (Grand Rapids, MI: Zondervan, 1985), 370.
4. Herman Melville, *Moby Dick*, chap. 9.
5. John Calvin, *Commentaries on the Twelve Minor Prophets,* trans. John Owen; from comments on Jonah 1:7.
6. Melville, *Moby Dick*, chap. 9.
7. Ellison, *Jonah*, 372.
8. Calvin, *Commentaries*, Jonah 1:11–12.
9. Jerome H. Smith, *The New Treasury of Scripture Knowledge* (Nashville: Nelson, 1992), 990.
10. C. S. Lewis, *Surprised by Joy* (New York: Harcourt Brace, 1955), 220–21.
11. Francis Thompson, "The Hound of Heaven" (1908).
12. Lewis, *Surprised by Joy,* 221.
13. "And Can It Be," Charles Wesley (1738).
14. Timothy Keller, *The Reason for God* (New York: Dutton, 2008), 177.

SCENE 2
1. From the *Publishers Weekly* review (1989) of *Albert Pinkham Ryder: Painter of Dreams* by William Innes Homer and Lloyd Goodrich (New York: Abrams, 1989), as quoted at http://www.amazon.com (accessed April 20, 2009).
2. From "Albert Pinkham Ryder," *The History of Art and the Curious Lives of Painters,* http://www.historyofpainters.com/albert_pinkham.htm (accessed April 20, 2009).
3. Lynn R. Huber, Dan W. Clanton Jr., and Jane S. Webster, "Biblical Subjects in Art," in *Teaching the Bible through Popular Culture and the Arts,* ed. Mark Roncace and Patrick Gray (Atlanta: Society of Biblical Literature, 2007), 202.
4. Homer and Goodrich, *Albert Pinkham Ryder*, 16.
5. The painting *Jonah* by Albert Pinkham Ryder is in the National Museum of American Art in Washington DC.
6. From *Albert Pinkham Ryder* by Frederic Fairchild Sherman (New York: private printing, 1920), 49.
7. John Calvin, *Commentaries on the Twelve Minor Prophets,* trans. John Owen; from comments on Jonah 1:17.
8. Joyce Baldwin, "Jonah," in *The Minor Prophets*, vol. 2, ed. Thomas Edward McComiskey (Grand Rapids, MI: Baker, 1993), 566.
9. Wayne Grudem, *Systematic Theology* (Leicester, UK: Inter-Varsity, 1994), 326.
10. Calvin, *Commentaries*, Jonah 1:17.
11. Dennis McGeary, *Jonah*, viewed at GalleryMcGeary.com, http://www.gallerymcgeary.com/abstract4.html (accessed April 24, 2009).
12. Thomas T. Perowne, *Obadiah and Jonah* (Cambridge: Cambridge University Press, 1889), 73.
13. Charles H. Spurgeon, "Salvation of the Lord" (sermon 131), preached at the Music Hall, Royal Surrey Gardens, May 10, 1857.
14. Douglas Stuart, *Hosea–Jonah*, Word Biblical Commentary, vol. 31 (Waco, TX: Word, 1987), 478.
15. Ibid.

A NEW BEGINNING
1. Joyce Baldwin, "Jonah," in *The Minor Prophets*, vol. 2, ed. Thomas Edward McComiskey (Grand Rapids, MI: Baker, 1993), 574.
2. A marble sculpture of Jonah was designed and guided by Raphael then finished by Lorenzetto around 1520 and is in the Chigi Chapel of the Church of Santa Maria del Popolo, Rome.

3. Phillip Ratner's *Jonah* sculpture is at the Dennis and Phillip Ratner Museum in Bethesda, MD; viewed at http://www.ratnermuseum.com/?page=heroes# (accessed April 28, 2009).

4. Pieter Lastman (1583–1633), *Jonah and the Whale*; James Tissot (1836–1902), *Jonah*, Jewish Museum, New York; Salvador Dali (1904–1989), *Jonah and the Whale*; Wayne Forte, *Lifeline: Jonah* (2002). All are included in the image collection entitled, "How Jonah Left the Fish: Jonah 2:11 in Art" by Klaas Spronk, EABS, Lisbon, at Scribd.com; http://www.scribd.com/doc/8952724/How-Jonah-Left-the-Fish (accessed April 25, 2009).

5. H. L. Ellison, *Jonah*, Expositor's Bible Commentary (EBC), vol. 7 (Grand Rapids, MI: Zondervan, 1985), 379.

6. "For I will forgive their iniquity, and I will remember their sin no more" (Jer. 31:34); "You will cast all our sins into the depths of the sea" (Mic. 7:19); "As far as the east is from the west, so far does he remove our transgressions from us" (Ps. 103:12).

7. Dan B. Allender, *Leading with a Limp: Turning Your Struggles into Strengths* (Colorado Springs, CO: WaterBrook, 2006) n.p.

8. Isaac Watts, "Alas! And Did My Savior Bleed?" Also known as "At the Cross" (1707).

SCENE 3

1. John Calvin, *Commentaries on the Twelve Minor Prophets*, trans. John Owen; from comments on Jonah 3:1–3.

2. Regarding Nineveh's greatness, Douglas Stuart translates the phrase in 3:3 this way: "Now, Nineveh was a city important to God." He comments: "The emphasis placed on Nineveh is not primarily in terms of its physical size but its *importance* to God. . . . The basic issue goes beyond Nineveh's sheer bulk to its intrinsic value to God." Douglas Stuart, *Hosea–Jonah*, Word Biblical Commentary, vol. 31 (Waco, TX: Word, 1987), 437, 481.

3. Dale M. Brown, *Mesopotamia: The Mighty Kings* (New York: Time-Life Books, 1995), 17.

4. Ibid., 24.

5. Cyrus Herzl Gordon, Meir Lubetski, et al., *Boundaries of the Ancient Near Eastern World* (Sheffield, UK: Sheffield Academic Press, 1998), 386.

6. See Stuart, *Hosea–Jonah*, 440; and H. L. Ellison, *Jonah*, Expositor's Bible Commentary (EBC), vol. 7 (Grand Rapids, MI: Zondervan, 1985), 361.

7. Charles H. Spurgeon, "War! War! War!" (sermon 250), preached at the Music Hall, Royal Surrey Gardens, May 1, 1859.

8. Gerard Hoet's illustration of Jonah in Nineveh is from *Figures de la Bible* (The Hague: Pierre deHondt, 1728).

9. Ellison, *Jonah*, 381.

10. Some scholars think the "king of Nineveh" mentioned in Jonah 3 must be the local ruler over the city rather than the king of the Assyrian Empire, especially since it appears that Calah, rather than Nineveh, was Assyria's official capital at this time. But Stuart comments: "It is . . . quite likely that Nineveh functioned as a royal residence, even if not the capital technically, during most of the eighth century BC. . . . It is clear that Nineveh became at least *de facto* the chief city of the neo-Assyrian Empire and host to royalty during much of that period" (*Hosea–Jonah*, 442). Ellison states that the issue of the king's identity is essentially "irrelevant" (*Jonah*, 383).

11. Calvin, *Commentaries*, Jonah 3:6–8.

12. Ellison, *Jonah*, 383.

13. Calvin, *Commentaries*, Jonah 3:6–8.

14. Ellison, *Jonah*, 383.

15. See Leland Ryken, Jim Wilhoit, et al., *Dictionary of Biblical Imagery* (Downers Grove, IL: InterVarsity, 1998), 329. Also: "Introduction to Jonah," in *The ESV Study Bible* (Wheaton, IL: Crossway, 2008), 1685.

16. G. K. Chesterton, *Orthodoxy* (London: John Lane, 1909), 34–35.

17. Alexander Maclaren, "Commentary on Matthew 12:41," in *Expositions of Holy Scripture: St. Matthew Chaps. IX to XXVIII*, repr. ed. (Charleston, SC: BiblioBazaar, 2006), 183.

18. As reported by Rachel Zoll, AP Religion Writer, in *USA Today,* April 1, 2008, http://www.usatoday.com/news/nation/2008-04-01-317252004_x.htm (accessed May 10, 2009).

19. Michael S. Horton, *Too Good to Be True: Finding Hope in a World of Hype* (Grand Rapids, MI: Zondervan, 2006), 23.

20. From the hymn "Hallelujah! What a Savior!" by Philip P. Bliss (1875).

21. Cornelius Plantinga, *Not the Way It's Supposed to Be: A Breviary of Sin* (Grand Rapids, MI: Eerdmans, 1995), "Vandalism of Shalom," title of chapter 1.

SCENE 4

1. In God's description of Nineveh in the opening verses of the book of Jonah, Douglas Stuart prefers to translate this Hebrew word as "trouble" rather than "wickedness": "Their trouble is of concern to me." He comments, "God is as concerned about Nineveh's miseries as he is angry at its evils." Douglas Stuart, *Hosea–Jonah*, Word Biblical Commentary, vol. 31 (Waco, TX: Word, 1987), 437, 444.

2. H. L. Ellison, *Jonah*, Expositor's Bible Commentary (EBC), vol. 7 (Grand Rapids, MI: Zondervan, 1985), 385.

3. Stuart, *Hosea–Jonah*, 503.

4. James Wolfendale, *Homiletical Commentary on the Minor Prophets* (London: Richard D. Dickinson, 1879), 385.

5. John Calvin, *Commentaries on the Twelve Minor Prophets,* trans. John Owen; from comments on Jonah 4:4.

6. Ellison, *Jonah*, 386.

7. *New Geneva Study Bible,* ed. R. C. Sproul (Nashville: Thomas Nelson, 1995), note on Jonah 2:1–10.

8. C. S. Lewis, *The Great Divorce* (1946; repr. New York: HarperCollins, 2001), 106.

9. From "How Can I Know God?" (June 1991) http://download.redeemer com/pdf/learn/resources/How_Can_I_Know_God-Keller.pdf (accessed April 25, 2009).

10. Augustine, *Confessions,* bk. 1, sec. 1.

SCENE 5

1. Janet Howe Gaines, *Forgiveness in a Wounded World: Jonah's Dilemma* (Atlanta: Society of Biblical Literature, 2003), 126.

2. Marble sarcophagus from Italy (c. 290), now in the Bode Museum, Berlin, Germany; http://www.sacred-destinations.com/germany/berlin-bode-museum-photos/slides/ xti_7147p.php (accessed May 3, 2009).

3. "The Jonah Window," designed by Abraham van Linge in the 1630s, in Christ Church Cathedral, Oxford, England; http://www.sacred-destinations.com/england/ oxford-christ-church-pictures/slides/can_005_detail.htm (accessed April 30, 2009).

4. Eugen Spiro (1874–1972), *Jonah,* in the "Prophetic Men" series; http://www.superstock. co.uk/stock-photos-images/900-9455 (accessed May 1, 2009).

5. Gaines, *Forgiveness*, 126.

6. H. L. Ellison, *Jonah*, Expositor's Bible Commentary (EBC), vol. 7 (Grand Rapids, MI: Zondervan, 1985), 390.

7. Ibid.

8. Douglas Stuart, *Hosea–Jonah*, Word Biblical Commentary, vol. 31 (Waco, TX: Word, 1987), 508.
9. Thomas T. Perowne, *Obadiah and Jonah* (Cambridge: Cambridge University Press, 1889), 91.
10. Stuart, *Hosea–Jonah*, 435.
11. Jerry Bridges, *Transforming Grace* (Colorado Springs, CO: NavPress, 1991), 70.

THE LARGER SCENE

1. G. K. Beale, *We Become What We Worship: A Biblical Theology of Idolatry* (Downers Grove, IL: IVP Academic, 2008), 17.
2. Timothy Keller, *The Prodigal God* (New York: Dutton, 2008), 15–16
3. Leo Tolstoy, *A Confession*, chap. 5.
4. Jerry Bridges, *The Gospel in Real Life* (Colorado Springs, CO: NavPress, 2002), 11.
5. Jerry Bridges, *Transforming Grace* (Colorado Springs, CO: NavPress, 1991), 11–12.
6. *Rocky* (1976), screenplay by Sylvester Stallone.
7. C. S. Lewis, *The Four Loves* (New York: Harcourt Brace Jovanovich, 1960), 169.

THE LATER SCENES

1. C. T. Fritsch, "Nineveh," *International Standard Bible Encyclopedia*, vol. 3 (Grand Rapids, MI: Eerdmans, 1986), 541.
2. See Joel 1:14–16, 18; 2:1–2, 12–13.
3. Douglas Stuart, *Hosea–Jonah*, Word Biblical Commentary, vol. 31 (Waco, TX: Word, 1987), 479
4. Ibid., 432.
5. John Piper, *Jonah* (Parts 1, 2, and 3); http://www.desiringgod.org/ResourceLibrary/Poems (accessed May 5, 2009).
6. Robert Frost, *A Masque of Mercy* (New York: Henry Holt, 1947); as reprinted in *The Poetry of Robert Frost*, ed. Edward Connery Lathem (New York: Holt, Rinehart and Winston, 1969), 493–521.
7. Nancy Nahra, "God of Our Yankees: The Evolution of God in Robert Frost," in *Forum on Public Policy [Online]: A Journal of the Oxford Round Table*, Summer2008;http://www.forumonpublicpolicy.com/summer08papers/archive summer08/nahra.pdf (accessed April 30, 2009).
8. Stuart, *Hosea–Jonah*, 443.

GENERAL INDEX

SCRIPTURE INDEX